Balloons on the Mailbox

Balloons on the Mailbox

◆

One Mother's Heartbreaking Story of Her Daughter's Death

Chantal D. Hørup
Inspired by Jacqueline Olivia Hørup

iUniverse, Inc.
New York Lincoln Shanghai

Balloons on the Mailbox
One Mother's Heartbreaking Story of Her Daughter's Death

Copyright © 2007 by Chantal D. Hørup

All rights reserved. No part of this book may be used or reproduced by any means, graphic, electronic, or mechanical, including photocopying, recording, taping or by any information storage retrieval system without the written permission of the publisher except in the case of brief quotations embodied in critical articles and reviews.

iUniverse books may be ordered through booksellers or by contacting:

iUniverse
2021 Pine Lake Road, Suite 100
Lincoln, NE 68512
www.iuniverse.com
1-800-Authors (1-800-288-4677)

Because of the dynamic nature of the Internet, any Web addresses or links contained in this book may have changed since publication and may no longer be valid.

The views expressed in this work are solely those of the author and do not necessarily reflect the views of the publisher, and the publisher hereby disclaims any responsibility for them.

ISBN: 978-0-595-44572-1 (pbk)
ISBN: 978-0-595-69052-7 (cloth)
ISBN: 978-0-595-88898-6 (ebk)

Printed in the United States of America

In loving memory of
Jacqueline Olivia Hørup

Contents

Preface ix
Acknowledgments xi

CHAPTER 1   Chantal 1
    London 1
    A Baby 4
    Jacqueline Is Coming 6

CHAPTER 2   My World Came Crashing Down 12
    Time of Death 12
    State of Shock 13
    Meeting Jacqueline 17
    Words of Wisdom 21

CHAPTER 3   Going Home Empty-handed 22
    Telling Veronique 22
    The Poem 23
    Unwavering Support 24
    The Funeral 25
    Defense Mechanism 29

CHAPTER 4   Life Must Go On 31
    Ken's Return to Work 31
    Thank-you Cards 31
    Putting Her Possessions Away 32
    Autopsy Results 34
    My First Visit to Savannah 35

CHAPTER 5   Remembering Does Help 39
    My Outlet 39
    Veronique Looking Out the Window 40

Chapter 6	Dare to Compare	42
	Losing Ella	42
	Bel and Me	45
	The Drink	48
Chapter 7	Starting to Heal	50
	Cemetery Visit	50
	People Who Do Not Know	51
	Offering Her Possessions as Gifts	53
	The Letter	54
Chapter 8	Helping Others	56
	Christiana	56
	Another Loss	64
Chapter 9	Therapy Helps	66
	A Vacation	66
	Second Guessing	68
Chapter 10	Here We Go Again	71
	Preparing for a Son	71
	Honesty Comes from Children	73
Chapter 11	As Times Goes By	74
	One-year Anniversary	74
	My Father	77
	Reminders	79
	Signs	82
Chapter 12	Another Birth	86
	Tristan's Delivery	86
	Veronique Met Her Brother	89
	God's Natural Drug	90
	Christina's Birthday	92
Conclusion		95
Quotes		97

Preface

In June 2004, I lost my baby girl in the first moments of her life on this earth. I spent the following weeks immobilized under a mountain of devastation, loss, and grief. Day by day, I searched for an air pocket under all that rubble—a lifeline—or something that could breathe some life back into me. Family and friends didn't know what to say. How could they know?

I found that the people who loved us the most were at a loss for words and actions. They felt helpless. All they wanted to know was what they could do for us. They simply did not know what to do or say. Yet the taboo against speaking of the loss of a child makes losing a baby even more unbearable to its parents. Experiencing my own grief, I wondered how I would survive through all its different stages.

Because of my recent experience supporting a friend after the loss of her newborn infant, helping her to understand her own feelings and realize that she was not alone, I felt that it was my duty to share my personal story with others too. I began with just writing a few pages to send to local hospitals and birthing centers. But I eventually wrote this book, in hopes of getting my story out there to help parents and their friends deal with the loss of a child.

My hope is that I can help you.

Acknowledgments

First, I want to thank my loving husband, Ken, for his faithful support during the long hours and weekends I devoted to writing my book. His unwavering encouragement allowed me to produce this book, of which I am very proud.

My sister, Francine, has been an instrumental part of this process by being extremely supportive in helping me create my dream. Without her words of wisdom in those early days, I am not certain I would have accomplished this result.

Bel, for always being available, on a whim, to read, reread, evaluate, edit, and give awesome suggestions throughout this process.

Amy, for dropping everything on more than one occasion to lend her ear and give invaluable advice.

Heather, for believing in my talent before I realized it myself and for pushing me to write my story.

Michelle, for her never-ending resourcefulness and tireless assistance with the technical aspects of publishing my book.

To all my friends and family members, too numerous to mention, I must thank you from the bottom of my heart. I appreciate, more than words can say, that you took the time to read my initial scribbles, offering valuable input and encouragement throughout.

1

Chantal

London

There I was, twenty-two years old, single and bored. Life had to be more than just mindlessly working during the day with occasional outings in the evenings, right? A change was needed—some excitement too. What I really needed was to find my soul mate. So I traveled to find him.

How would I shake up my life? Should I follow my friend Linda's footsteps? Her life seemed so glamorous. She was living abroad, married to an Englishman. "How cool," I thought. That had become my dream. I painstakingly saved up what I considered a small fortune and purchased a ticket to London, England. My plan was to visit Linda and her wonderful husband, David. They had graciously invited me into their home. My plan was to use it as my home base and then travel across Europe. Once my decision had been made, my excitement was palpable. The thought of going where nobody knew my name was very enticing.

November 14, 1990, was the day I started my new life. As I came off the Jetway at the Gatwick International Airport in England, I felt a mixture of excitement and terror. As promised, Linda met me at the gate, where I immediately felt welcomed and overjoyed at seeing her smiling face. Within seconds, her smile faded as she noticed the amount of luggage I was toting. I had to haul my two huge, old-fashioned suitcases, without modern wheels, up and down escalators and stairwells as we made our way to the train station. Hiring a cab to travel back to London was out of the question. Who could afford that? I had no idea how far we were from my new home, and already I had felt exhausted.

Shortly after we settled ourselves in our seats on the train, a beverage cart came around. I was starving and thirsty, so I ordered a Coke.

"May I have some ice, please?" I politely asked, because the beverage was lukewarm.

"He does not have ice, Chantal," Linda knowingly stated, with laughter in her voice. I felt like I was in another world.

"How can they possibly serve this beverage warm?" I wondered aloud.

That was one of my first reality checks. The English simply do not care for ice. Who knew? My second reality check was just how expensive England was. Just the cost of my Coke took me by surprise. I immediately realized that my money was not going to take me far. What I needed was a job, especially if I wanted to stay in London for a while and travel too. After a few days of visiting museums, parks, and art galleries in that great city, it was time to start searching for a job.

I am French Canadian. Being a Canadian citizen was all I had needed to apply for a "holidaymaker working visa." That visa was to allow me to work anywhere in the United Kingdom for up to two years. Having it stamped in my passport, I decided to use it. How hard would it be to find employment there? I thought that being bilingual would help too. The way I figured it, I would work a little and then travel a little. Having previously worked in various retail stores, I had a very high opinion of myself as a salesperson as well as a manager. Therefore, my very first stop was at the world-renowned Harrods department store. After putting on the classiest outfit I had packed, I made my grand entrance into the highly esteemed establishment. The very first person I saw steered me toward the HR department to request a job application. As I mechanically filled it out, I wondered which department they would assign me to. They would probably let me pick, I assumed. How naive I was.

I honestly thought I was God's gift to Harrods and that I would be hired on the spot, without even the degrading need to be interviewed. I fell back to earth very fast when they did not even call me for an interview. They were simply not interested in my services! I was stunned. Day after day, I wore my best suit and walked the beautiful streets of London, Piccadilly Circus, Oxford Street, and Regent Street, searching for a job, any job. At that point, I was applying at any place of business with a "help wanted" sign—if I had the guts to enter, that is. Finally, feeling pretty low, I decided to resort to applying at various restaurants. How thrilled was I when, after applying at Pizza Hut, I was finally hired on the spot as a server! I was to begin orientation the very next day.

When I walked into the restaurant for my first shift, the manager introduced me to a Danish man named Ken. He asked Ken to show me the ropes. Ken had been working at Pizza Hut for a few months by then, but I quickly realized that his English was very poor. He was, in fact, in England for the sole purpose of learning to speak English. He was to return to Denmark with his newly acquired skills, better equipped to further his education. We worked side by side without so much as a glance at each other until one day, a few months later.

"Does anyone want to play tennis?" I asked, as I walked into the staff room.

Ken was there, and he nodded, meaning, "I do."

I wondered if we should even bother getting together, because he still barely spoke English. We made a date anyway, to meet the next day at a neighborhood tennis court.

That was the best decision of my life! We played tennis for hours and then went out for a beer at one of London's famous landmarks, the Hard Rock Café. It was as if a giant light bulb had turned on in my head as soon as we walked into the café. I looked over at Ken, sitting next to me on the bar stool with the shimmering lights shining down on him, and I just fell in love with him that very moment. From that day on, we were inseparable. We began dating, and in no time at all, we had decided to make our life together. We began planning our future and spent endless nights discussing how we wanted our lives to move forward.

We had many hurdles to overcome, the main one being logistics. After all, my days in England were numbered. Were we to return to Canada or Denmark? On the other hand, should we choose a neutral country like the United States? Ken's parents expected their son to return to Denmark to finish his studies; he even had a return flight ticket in hand, as did I. Young and free, we decided to live one day at a time, enjoying just being together until a decision absolutely needed to be made.

That was such a magical time for Ken and me. We managed to work similar schedules at Pizza Hut so that we could spend our free time walking the streets of London, hand in hand, becoming intimate in our knowledge of that amazing city. We knew where to find the best pastries, the cheapest fish and chips, and the very best coffeehouses. We knew what streets to walk down to get to almost any park in London. What more did we need? Even with our language barrier, we discussed everything in our relationship. We were definitely a match made in heaven. I could not believe my luck. What a blessing! I knew, without a doubt, that I had found the perfect man for me. I wanted to spend the rest of my life with Ken.

We spent hours upon hours just talking about what we wanted to do in life, and finally we narrowed in on one of Ken's dreams. He wanted to become a chiropractor. From that moment on, we put all our energy into making it happen. We filled out his application to Life University in Marietta, Georgia, in the United States. We then anxiously awaited a response until, one day, an envelope from Life University arrived. We looked it over from every angle, speculating on its content. Eventually, we opened it and happily received our walking papers. Our adult lives were about to begin.

By the time we left London, I had been promoted in the Pizza Hut corporation to restaurant manager and had received a direct transfer from Pizza Hut International to Pizza Hut USA. They relocated me to a restaurant just a few miles from Ken's new school, in Smyrna, Georgia. Shortly after our arrival in the United States, Ken and I decided to make our union official. So, on a bright and sunny Tuesday in February 1993, we exchanged wedding vows in a very intimate ceremony. It was just the two of us, with the justice of the peace. We could not afford a serious wedding, and like so many young couples, we could not wait! A few months later, we celebrated our wedding with our families.

Blissfully happy, I continued working, first in the restaurant business and then in the chiropractic management business. During that time, Ken excelled at his studies, even though he was placed in "developmental English" class as soon as he started. After years of hard effort, he received his diploma in 1997. Like all of his graduating classmates, Ken asked; "What now?" We were slightly better equipped than many of them because I had made it my mission to learn everything necessary to run a successful chiropractic practice. So we were off, ready to start our own clinic.

With his chiropractic diploma in hand, we searched for a new place to call our home. Where did we see our life going? That is when a wonderful opportunity presented itself—to relocate to the beautiful, sunny island of Hilton Head in South Carolina. We moved to Hilton Head Island and worked long and hard to build a successful chiropractic clinic to sustain the lifestyle we had envisioned. Side by side, we worked for many years, succeeding in building our business. Then we decided to start a family.

A Baby

My Life Goals
- ☑ In love
- ☑ Have husband
- ☑ Have home
- ☑ Have vehicle
- ☑ Have friends
- ☑ Have career
- ☑ Financially secure
- ☐ Have baby

It seemed that I had it all planned out. I had everything I had ever wanted in life—and much more, actually. My husband, Ken, and I had come so far in a relatively short amount of time. We were planning our next move, in our life-size chess game. Strategically, we had arrived at a perfect time to start a family. More importantly, I had begun yearning for a baby. I was thirty-two years old, and my biological clock had begun ticking. We decided to go for it. We were ready to be parents. The excitement was palpable for both of us. Ken could not wait to teach soccer to his own children and buy mini soccer outfits too. I was looking forward to speaking French to our children and keeping as much of our heritage as possible.

"Do you need a license to be a parent?" we jokingly teased each other. Actually, Ken stated that he wanted us to take a parenting class, to prepare us for what was to come. Because neither of us had been raised with young children, we were unsure of the challenges that lay ahead. Unfortunately, we did not have time to take a parenting class; I became pregnant just a couple of months later.

Morning sickness began immediately. I was surprised, as I am a very healthy person, and the thought of feeling sick continually had never occurred to me. I was working full-time in our clinic and needed to be sitting at the front desk all day long. The nausea, often excruciating, was followed by being violently ill. I had to greatly rely on my co-worker Shelly. The horrible morning sickness felt like it lasted forever. However, it did not. By the fourth month, I was feeling like all my other pregnant friends—just plain fat!

Ken and I considered childbirth a natural experience; therefore, we decided to find a birthing center and a midwife to deliver our children. I wondered how I was going to find one and if they were listed like other obstetricians. When I searched the phone book, I was unable to find "birthing center" or "midwife group." When I dialed the local information number and asked the same question, there were none on file. As fate would have it, the operator I spoke to had used a birthing center in Savannah, Georgia—about one hour away from our home. She gave me the phone number, and I called to make an appointment.

When Ken and I visited the birthing center, it felt very homey. Furthermore, we saw that the birthing rooms were decorated just like normal, cozy bedrooms, with pretty bedspreads and curtains on the windows. There was even a living room area designed for family and visitors to use while waiting during labor. Immediately, a feeling of comfort enveloped us. There was also a large tub designed for underwater birth. That was exactly what we wanted, along with the availability of modern medical equipment, just in case. Ken and I were happy to learn that we were touring a Level 1 facility. That meant that the birthing center held the same level of accreditation as the hospital on Hilton Head Island. That was it. No more searching. We were very comfortable with what we saw. We made our decision; that was where our baby would be delivered.

Throughout my pregnancy, I received my prenatal care at the birthing center and met all the midwives. Ken and I were very excited about the upcoming birth of our first child. We had decided to keep the sex of our baby a mystery even to us, so the anticipation was unmistakable. As I continued to work in our clinic, patients continuously asked when we were expecting our bundle of joy. Was it to be a boy or a girl? That was to be a surprise—one of the best kinds.

We picked a name for a girl and one for a boy. Being French Canadian, I always want to keep a little French in my life, so we chose French names. For some reason, I started looking at the baby name book from the end. Names starting with a Z, X, and W were not very interesting, but I quickly became stuck on the V's. I loved so many of them. That is how we ended up with "Veronique." In our families, both in Canada and Denmark, no one puts much stock in middle names. Ken does not even have one. Therefore, for our first daughter's middle name, we chose something that Ken and I had always thought was charming: Kacey. K for Ken and C for Chantal.

How we chose that middle name is humorous, actually. We had often talked about getting a dog when we were just married. We had discussed at length what kind of dog it would be and especially what we would name the dog. We had had lots of time on our hands as young newlyweds without children. We had decided to call our first puppy Kacey. As luck would have it, our first dog found us! He seemed to be homeless, but neighbors told us that his name was Jackson. We called him once, just to see, and he came, so Jackson was to stay his name. After an unsuccessful search for his owner, we adopted Jackson. He lived with us for ten years. Since we did not use the name Kacey then, we decided to use it as Veronique's middle name.

When my contractions finally started on the evening of Monday, December 4, 2000, I was thrilled. We rushed to the birthing center, nervously wondering what we were in for. Veronique finally made her entrance into our world at 11:58 PM on December 5. She was born two weeks past her due date, I might add. After a twenty-eight hour labor, we welcomed our baby girl. Although my labor was long and hard, we had a wonderful experience at the birthing center. We also used the large tub to deliver our daughter underwater, and we were looking forward to using the same midwife group for a future pregnancy and delivery.

Driving home with our newborn was terrifying for Ken and me. Every noise she made was new; therefore, we constantly thought she was choking or, worse, not breathing. We could not wait to arrive home where we felt we would be safe. My mother was very happy to see us and took over as soon as we arrived. When my mother left seven days later, my good friend Keri found me crying in my pantry. It has since become a funny memory, but at the time, I was terrified that I would not be able to cope with my newborn. Keri was very helpful every step of the way during those days, because she herself had a six-month-old daughter, Emily.

I greatly enjoyed nursing Veronique, even though it was very time-consuming, as she continuously fell asleep while nursing. I used all the tricks in the book to keep her awake during her feedings. I became a pro! I nursed her well into her second year of life too. Since my sister, Francine, was the first in our family to have a child, I found myself relying on her expertise more times than I care to recall. As a result, Francine and I became closer and shared many good times together. Still, having a child to care for was constantly a challenge. Everything was new, exciting, and often terrifying. Ken and I had decided that we wanted to have two children, although when we would be ready for the second child was still a mystery.

Jacqueline Is Coming

I was anxious about undergoing another pregnancy. I was especially afraid of having morning sickness again, and I also hoped that this next labor would be faster and less painful. Having made the decision to use the same birthing center to deliver our second child meant that I was not going to be getting an epidural. I knew what to expect the second time. I will admit this is probably the reason I decided to wait a few years before having another child. Being in the chiropractic field, my husband and I try to use natural approaches to maintain our health. We practice a good balance between traditional medicine and natural medicine.

I am blessed with fertility, and before long, I was pregnant. It was such a magical time because several of my close friends, including my very best friend, Mabel, or Bel as she is known in our group, were also pregnant—Bel was just a few months ahead of me. We were excited that our children would share the same school year. We were looking forward to arranging photos of our newest additions in our family scrapbooks. As we had with our first daughters, we were already talking of our field trip to the Sears photography center and what adorable clothes the kids would wear. To top it off, my due date was one week before my niece's birthday. My sister, Francine, and I joked that it would be funny if the cousins had the same birthday.

Just like with my first pregnancy, it seemed that the morning sickness hit me the day I came back from the local drug store with my home pregnancy test in hand. Unfortunately, my second pregnancy was worse! I was so sick, that, early on in the first trimester, I needed to have an IV to rehydrate. Thankfully, my father and stepmother, escaping from the cold Montréal winters, were spending six months out of the year with us, living in our mother-in-law suite. This was very helpful while I was practically incapacitated.

Thankfully, as with my first pregnancy, from the fourth month on, I had a great pregnancy. I felt especially good toward the end.

With our second child, Ken just could not wait to find out what we were going to have—girl or boy. Once I knew we were going to find out the sex of our new baby, I also got very excited. Finally, I was going to know whether to decorate the baby's room with lots of pink or lots of blue. The ultrasound day came, and we found out that we were having another girl. Again, we looked at the baby name book. I was still stuck on the V's, but Ken did not agree this time. So we broadened our search and found a beautiful French name that I have loved forever—Jacqueline. This was the name of my aunt in Montréal, an aunt I really loved as a child. I dreamed of saying, "Veronique and Jacqueline, come here," or "Veronique and Jacqueline, Papa is home," or "Veronique and Jacqueline, dinner is ready …"

A search for a middle name ensued. What should we choose? We finally settled on Olivia, because we liked it. The reason I liked it, though, was that the Kennedy family had always fascinated me. Like so many women, I had been hypnotized over the years, watching Jackie O glide in and out of many social occasions. Simply hearing the name Jackie O could draw me into any conversation. If I heard a commentator speak her name, I would stop chasing a better program on TV. So I thought, "Why not find a middle name starting with an O so I can have my very own Jackie O?"

Everyone was asking me if I was looking forward to "unloading" the baby. Since my due date came and went without labor starting, my answer was always that she could stay there as long as she wanted, because I was sleeping well and spending a lot of time with Veronique, who was three and a half years old by then. I knew that as soon as Jacqueline came, I was going to have my hands full. Little did I know the horrible irony of these thoughts.

On Thursday, June 3, 2004, I started having contractions at 9:00 AM. I was one week past my due date, and I had an appointment with my midwife at 11:30 AM. I was excited. I called Francine to let her know the news that our girls would be sharing the same birthday.

"I'm going to the birthing center for my appointment, and I won't need to leave," I exclaimed to my mother that morning. She had arrived a few days before to help with our newborn. Like most mothers, mine loves babies. As we had done right before our last delivery, we packed some snacks to eat during the day, put them in my prepared overnight bag, and headed to the birthing center. Since we chose a natural approach to childbirth without the use of drugs, I was able to eat and drink throughout the labor.

I called Ken and told him that today was finally "the day," but, since our last labor had lasted so long, we decided that Ken could drive separately and finish seeing his last patients. My mother and I drove together, and Ken would be coming in another car. Throughout the drive to Savannah, I kept timing my contractions. They were coming five minutes apart, lasting forty-five seconds, and were not too painful. I then called Maureen, our longtime babysitter. Maureen was always ready and willing to be there for us. She promised to pick up Veronique after day care and keep her until my mother returned from the birthing center.

I was excited and happy when we arrived. The first person I saw was Vicky, a brand new employee, who was beaming with anticipation. She confided that this was to be her first birth.

"I can't wait to see your newborn baby!" she said happily.

I waited for a short while in the waiting room, hearing and seeing lots of mothers and babies. Shortly after arriving, I was escorted to one of the exam rooms where I saw Nancy, the midwife on duty that day. Ken and I had secretly hoped that Nancy would deliver our second child, and I was happy and relieved to see her. When she checked me, I was only 1 centimeter dilated. Remembering my last labor that lasted *forever*, we thought that maybe it was going to be a long haul again.

Since I was at forty-one weeks gestation, Nancy informed me that she needed to perform a stress test. For the test, I had to lie down on my back, with wires positioned on my belly. I needed to push a button every time I felt movement, such as a kick, from the baby. Being in an uncomfortable position, I started to have more frequent and more intense contractions. I had difficulties discerning the difference between a contraction and a kick. Mostly I was trying to stay somewhat comfortable.

At the end of the stress test, Nancy came in and looked at the readout results. She said that my results were out of the normal range, but due to the contractions, they were not "terribly abnormal" as she put it. She said we should see how quickly my labor progressed from there and that in one hour she might need to do another stress test. After the test, I was still comfortable enough to feel hungry, even though the contractions were coming faster. Because we were thinking that the labor would be another long haul, my mother and I left the center in search of some food and to take a walk to help jump-start the labor. Within thirty minutes, I was back in the center, because, all of a sudden, the contractions were one minute apart and lasting one minute, not to mention how intense they had become.

Ken had arrived, and we were all excited. My mother asked if she could stay and be part of the upcoming miracle of birth. We said yes. Nancy set me up in one of the birthing rooms, and I was slightly disappointed that I was not going to deliver my new baby in the same room I had delivered Veronique. Once we were all settled, Nancy checked me. I was 6 to 7 centimeters dilated, as I had progressed very quickly. It was approximately 1:00 PM. My labor was so much easier than the last one—much less painful and so much faster. I was very excited. My mother, camera in hand, took some happy pictures. Even through the contractions, I managed a smile. We were all chatting, eating our packed snacks, and listening to the heartbeat every five minutes. I had two midwives, one nurse, Ken, and my mother there with me.

When my water broke, there was meconium—the baby's first stool—in the bag. This occurrence is not highly unusual, although it is sometimes associated with fetal stress. No one was alarmed at that point, but because of the meconium, Nancy said I could not deliver the baby in the tub. They would have to aspirate the baby's lungs as soon as she came out, and the tub was too far from the machine. I was disappointed but did not really think about it much. I was just trying to get over the pain of the contractions, which were very intense by then.

Eventually it was time to push. Everything was going well. We continuously heard a strong heartbeat throughout. However, I was not pushing her out, so we took a small break from pushing. I was exhausted by then.

"Why isn't she coming out?" I asked to no one in particular. "Do you think I'm pushing hard enough?" I asked, aiming my question at Ken.

"No," he answered. For a second, I was annoyed, but, again, it's hard concentrating on anything but getting through the next contraction at that stage.

Shortly after, we resumed pushing, but after two hours of pushing, Nancy told me that if we did not get the baby out soon, I would have to be transported to the hospital. I did not want to move, because the pain was so intense. I got up to go to the bathroom and maybe try another position. When I returned to the bed, the nurse set the heartbeat monitor back on my tummy, and we searched for the heartbeat again but could not find it. Nancy calmly asked the nurse to go fetch a different monitor device, and finally we heard the heartbeat, but it was slower. It was at 100 instead of the usual 140–150. There was a slight concern. They immediately gave me oxygen, and using a much more forceful tone of voice, my midwife told me to push, and push hard. I did, and all of a sudden, her head came out. Everyone in the room was so excited.

"Look at how much hair she has," I heard someone say.

"Okay," I thought, "I can do this!"

With the next contraction, I pushed again, and her whole body came out. It was 6:22 PM. The clamp was attached onto the umbilical cord, and I think Ken cut it. I was overwhelmed that it was finally over. I am not sure my eyes were even open at that point. They immediately transported our baby to the aspiration machine. I just lay there, still catching my breath.

"You work on the baby; I'll work on the mom," Nancy calmly said to Jill, the other midwife. I was looking at Nancy as she spoke these words, and I noticed that she looked up at Jill. That is when Nancy left me. I caught a glimpse of my mother's facial expression, and I could not put my finger on what she was feeling or thinking, but I knew that something was not right. The amazing thing about the situation was that I was not concerned. I will never know why I was so much at peace during that time. I kept wondering, Why isn't she crying? So I looked over and saw them doing CPR on Jacqueline, but somehow, I did not hear much of the conversation.

Then I heard someone say, "Give her a dose of epi."

I remembered from watching one of my favorite television shows *ER* that epinephrine is a powerful drug used to jump-start the heart. That was not a good sign. I kept thinking, "She will cry soon; everything will be okay."

Nancy was calm, and everyone was working well; I sensed a high degree of competence from my team. I thought everything would be okay, because babies are strong. A baby can fall right on its head and be okay. On TV, you hear how even "crack babies" survive, right?

In a moment, my newborn baby girl was next to me, and the midwife asked me to talk to her.

I thought, "What do you mean? She's sleeping. She can't hear me."

The midwife nudged me gently and nodded her head. She was urging me to help Jacqueline wake up! As I had with Veronique, I began to speak softly to my new baby in French, encouraging her to wake up and open her eyes for me.

"Ouvre les yeux, ma poupoune! Reveille-toi!" I said softly.

During that time, Nancy was intubating Jacqueline. Apparently, the baby had a heartbeat of 20 at that point. That part is still blurry. I was still catching my breath and in a state of shock. I was sweating, yet I was shaking. I was about to say more to my beautiful baby when a team of paramedics arrived. I felt relief.

"Everything is going to be okay," I thought.

Then they began connecting several wires and machines to my newborn baby girl, trying to assess the situation, trying to save her. They could no longer find a heartbeat. They were desperately looking for her pulse, trying to feel if her heart was beating. They were looking at her skin tone, checking her vitals, and running through all the tests to determine her Apgar score. All of a sudden, my eyes found Ken. Tears were running down his cheeks as he followed the paramedics; he was leaving me to go with our daughter to the hospital. I just could not understand why he was crying.

I still had not delivered the placenta, and I needed sutures, so I could not go anywhere. Honestly, the thought of going anywhere did not even occur to me.

2

My World Came Crashing Down

Time of Death

As soon as Jacqueline was born, Ken knew there was a problem. He saw no life, no movement. He saw that she did not cry, even her tiny fingers did not move. He felt that Jacqueline came into this world looking like a doll, beautiful but not real.

What could he have done to change this outcome? He felt that she would not make it, because there was no heartbeat and no breathing. He knew that meant no life.

These thoughts and more were swimming in Ken's head as he and the paramedics made their way out to the ambulance, carefully transporting our baby girl. The sirens were blaring when they took off. The drive to the hospital took an eternity. Naturally, we think ambulances zoom through traffic with their sirens screaming while everyone gets out of the way, but the scary truth is that they spend most of their time just trying to get around other vehicles. Their goal is to try to get to their destination intact and as quickly as possible. The longer it took, the more final Ken knew our outcome would be.

When they arrived at the emergency room entrance, there was a team of doctors ready to work. Ken felt like he was in a nightmare. He remained clearheaded, but his emotions were out of control, and he sobbed hysterically as he never had before. Ken watched several competent doctors take control and start to work on our baby girl. The nursing staff asked him to go sit in another room to try to pull himself together. There, he sat alone for a few minutes, but he realized that he could not get any more composed sitting in a separate room. So he went back into the emergency room to watch as the doctors worked heroically to bring her back to life. They knew what to do and worked very efficiently.

Ken stood there alone with no direct support and no guidance. No one told him to talk to Jacqueline, to whisper I love you in her ear, to hold her hand … he stood there, sobbing.

He watched as the doctors made their final attempt to bring her back to life, knowing there was nothing else they could do. He then heard the final words—words he has since replayed in his mind over, and over again.

"Time of death: 19:55," Dr. Wright announced.

Ken was then escorted out of the emergency room to a different area. There, he sat alone again, just sobbing. The doctor in charge, Dr. Wright, came in to talk to him. He was nicely stating facts, being very professional. Through his sobs, Ken managed to ask him if the umbilical cord had wrapped itself around Jacqueline's neck and squeezed the life out of her when they had asked me to push harder. The doctor categorically said no. Ken was just looking for answers. How could things have gone so wrong? Would she have survived if I had given birth in a hospital? What if I would have had a C-section instead? He wondered if it was his fault. Oh, God! Could he have prevented the outcome? Ken continued to have these awful thoughts, and he could not stop sobbing.

Ken informed the doctor that I would be coming to the hospital soon, and Dr. Wright said he would be available to talk to us together when I arrived.

Eventually, a priest came in and tried to support Ken as best as he could. He tried to answer his basic question.

"Why did God do this?" Ken asked.

"God works in mysterious ways ..." was the priest's answer.

At that very moment, Ken could not say, in all honesty, that the priest's answer was helpful.

Shortly after, a nurse came into the room and asked if Ken wanted to see Jacqueline. He said yes, and they brought her in. They left him alone in the room with our little Jacqueline. Ken did not know what to do. He had never envisioned himself sitting with his dead daughter in his arms. Who does? Something like this could never happen. The hospital staff was nice, of course, but they did not offer him support or guidance. Therefore, he sat alone, looking at our daughter in his arms and sobbing as he asked for a phone to call me.

State of Shock

There have been periods in my life when I have found it necessary to get through some hard times. I have learned that the best way to deal with hard times is to not feel. Numbness and detachment are my most effective and powerful defense mechanisms. I mastered them well a long time ago. As I think back to those horrible hours after delivering my second daughter, I believe I subconsciously reverted to my old ways. This is, possibly, what kept me sane ...

I was in shock. What a powerful reaction. Unless you have experienced it yourself, you will never fully understand what shock can do to a person. For me, it was a godsend. Without it, I'm not sure how I would have survived the initial moments after Jacqueline's birth.

After Ken left the birthing center with the paramedics, I stayed in bed, wondering what was going on. I asked Nancy, my midwife, what she thought was wrong with Jacqueline. She said she did not know yet but that there might be something wrong with her heart. That is all I heard. I asked for a phone to call one of my best friends, Amy, whose dad is a cardiac surgeon. I figured she could help.

"I need your visualization powers, Amy," I said. I told her that Jacqueline was not breathing, that we did not know why, and that it may be her heart. I know I spoke as if this was happening to someone else, some stranger; I spoke with very little emotion. She was devastated upon hearing my news. I told her that Ken had just left with the baby in an ambulance for the hospital and asked her to meet him there. I told her that Ken was there alone and was not doing well, and she said she was on her way.

Amy later shared with me that she then called her mom and our friend Shelly to tell them we needed them to pray for Jacqueline. They told her they would.

I vaguely remember calling Maureen, Veronique's babysitter, to tell her that something was wrong with the baby. I asked her to pray for Jacqueline. Again, my level of shock was unbelievable, as I began concerning myself with the logistics of my first daughter. I knew that Maureen had a previous engagement that evening and that my mother was supposed to be home to relieve her, but my mother could not leave the birthing center.

"Could you drive Veronique to Suzanne's house?" I asked. My good friend Suzanne had previously offered her help. So, after speaking to her on the phone, it was arranged. Veronique would stay in their home for an overnight visit.

Years after these events, I talked with Suzanne about our conversation that day. She told me that after hanging up the phone that evening, she told her husband about the phone call.

"Chantal has absolutely no idea what has happened!" she told him in disbelief. Apparently, the manner in which I had shared my information and made my request was completely emotionless, leaving her to believe that I must be in a state of either shock or denial. In all honesty, I don't even remember making the call.

During that time, my mother was reacting to our terrible situation in the birthing center living room. I later found out that she had called my sister, Francine.

"It's not going well. Jacqueline is not breathing," my mother whispered into the phone.

"What? How is Chantal? What's happening?" Francine screamed into the phone. Apparently, my mother was very calm on the phone. Francine thought that our mother was disoriented and a little in shock too—that maybe she could not quite grasp what was happening and certainly did not seem to know what to do. She explained that Jacqueline had not taken a breath, and the medical staff was working on her and that Jacqueline had been sent to the hospital with Ken.

"Where is Chantal?" Francine asked. She answered that I was there, in bed, and she was not sure if I knew or understood what was happening. Francine immediately told her that I needed to be with the baby. My mother answered that I could not be moved.

It seems that, during their conversation, Ken had called my cell phone. He was sobbing, needing to tell me words I definitely was not ready to hear. With the phone to my ear, I listened on.

"Jacqueline didn't make it," he said. He went on to say that a team of twenty doctors and surgeons had worked on her for forty minutes or so. She had been pronounced dead at 7:55 PM. I could not react. I was numb. I did not cry.

"She didn't make it? Wow! Really? I can't believe she didn't make it," I repeated robotically, over and over. Maybe I knew, deep down, because I was almost not surprised, yet I still could not believe it. Nancy stayed by my side as Ken continued to speak. I told him that I had called Amy, and that she was on her way.

"Why Amy? She's pregnant! Why not Bruce?" Ken exclaimed. He thought she should not be put in this kind of situation. I told him that I thought something was wrong with Jacqueline's heart and that maybe Amy would know what questions to ask. I knew that I could count on her and that she would help just by being there. Ken was sobbing. He said he would call back in a few minutes. After we got off the phone, I realized that I had completely forgotten that Amy was pregnant and had only thought of the fact that her father could help if it was a heart problem. Again, I think, deep down, I knew there was no helping Jacqueline at that point. I am not sure about my reasoning. I then started to feel really bad about having called her, so I decided to call Amy back.

"She didn't make it," I flatly said.

"What? What do you mean she didn't make it?" she adamantly asked.

"Don't bother coming, because the baby did not make it!" I repeated. (I could not utter the word "died"). In my warped mind, I thought I was fixing my mistake of asking Amy to come by telling her not to come.

Amy categorically said that she was coming anyway. I did not have the energy to say anything further, so I simply said okay.

I understood from Ken's call that he would probably like to have our good friend Bruce there with him, so I called him too. I do not remember making that call. I do wonder what Bruce was thinking when I bluntly stated that our daughter had died and that Ken needed him.

After that call, I lay in bed, staring at the ceiling, quietly feeling absolutely nothing. That is when Ken called back and asked me to come to the hospital. He wanted me to see our baby. In a daze, I said I would try to leave very soon.

"Are you leaving in ten minutes?" Ken asked.

I thought, "Why rush?"

"I'm coming soon," I said. I was so tired; I wanted to close my eyes. "Why should I rush to the hospital to see my dead baby?" I thought. Why had Ken asked me to leave in ten minutes? "If nothing else, maybe I should go to be with my husband; he's distraught," I thought. I tried to get out of bed, but my legs simply would not obey! I could not make myself move. I was not paralyzed. I had not even had an epidural! Why did my legs not want to obey my brain's command?

When I think back to that time, I cannot believe that I could not move. Come on! Why not? Maybe I did not want to. I lay in bed for hours without crying or even fighting back tears. I am not even sure if I was sad at that moment. I knew I should be, but I could not feel anything.

I asked Nancy why I could not move. I do not remember her answer except that she said I should rest. As a result, I did not try to move again.

Somewhere in the distance, I heard my cell phone ringing. My mother was talking on the phone, but I couldn't have cared less what was being said. I have very little recollection of the conversation; therefore, I will rely on my sister's recollection.

"You need to get Chantal transported to that hospital by ambulance," Francine told our mother adamantly. It seems that my mother did not know what to do with that information. In her generation, when a baby died, you were supposed to forget about it or pretend it did not happen. I think she might have thought it was not a great idea for me to go to the hospital.

Francine later told me that she knew she needed to speak to someone who could make things happen, but she did not have Ken's phone number, nor would she have been comfortable enough to tell him what to do. She just did not know if it was her place to insist on having me transferred to the hospital to be by my baby's side. "This decision is seriously personal," she thought.

My mother walked toward me, extending her hand, offering the phone. Francine wanted to talk to me. After asking me how I was feeling and realizing that I was not in a normal frame of mind, she tried to help me understand that I should go to the hospital. Apparently, I told her that I was tired, I could not move my body, and I wanted to sleep.

"Maybe you could go by ambulance," she gently insisted. She told me that it was very important that I go to Jacqueline as soon as possible. Realistically, she knew that Jacqueline would be cold and stiff the next day, but she could not bring herself to tell me that.

"She won't be the same tomorrow," she tried to tell me. Francine continues to feel that, looking back on it now and many times immediately afterward, she regrets not insisting more.

"Francine, I want to sleep now," I said. I apparently just hung up the phone.

One of the midwives, Jill, had brought her own homemade banana bread for a snack. Our snacks were gone by then, and believe it or not, I was hungry. She offered her banana bread to my mother and me. As I ate the banana bread, I kept asking my mother and Nancy what I was going to tell Veronique when I returned home without her sister. Veronique was so excited about having a sister. She told everybody she met that she was going to be a big sister. I remember her speaking to complete strangers in the supermarket, telling them that her sister's name was Jacqueline. No matter where we were, she would come to me and lift up whatever T-shirt I was wearing and kiss my swollen belly, saying, "I love my sister!" I felt like a huge failure. I felt like I had lied to my daughter and that she would never believe a word I would say from then on.

That is what I thought about for hours, while I was lying in bed, trying to will my legs to move. "What am I going to do? What am I going to say? Can I make it through this?" I wondered. Let me add here that, at one point, I felt a need to go to the bathroom and still could not get up, so I peed in bed. My midwife team was very understanding and simply cushioned me with extra towels and cleaned me off as best they could. Nancy repeated that she was there if I wanted to try to get up again.

It was very odd what went through my mind at that time. I kept thinking of everyone who would be affected by our loss. I felt sorry for Vicky, the new employee from the birthing center. Mine was to be her first birthing experience, and I had ruined it. I also thought of Liz, one of the longtime staff members at our clinic. She had left for a vacation just a few days before. This young woman's smile can light up a room. With a huge smile, she had said that she was looking forward to her return, as she couldn't wait to meet our daughter. I thought of her as I lay in bed, staring at the ceiling. I felt like I was going to disappoint her too. And then I thought of Bel. She was on vacation with her family. I knew that my news would affect her tremendously. She is the second person I remember calling. Her cell phone rang. When she answered it, I knew immediately that, somehow, she already knew, as her voice was hoarse.

"The baby didn't make it," I said.

"I know. We're on our way home," she said. That vacation was cut short. I knew then that Bel cared—she cared a great deal.

Finally, Ken came back to the birthing center, after arranging for us to return to the hospital the next morning so I could see Jacqueline. I was already asleep when he came in, but I heard him arrive. I remained where I was, just wanting to escape back into blissful, mind-altering, mind-numbing sleep. And, unbelievably, I slept fairly well; unfortunately, Ken did not.

Meeting Jacqueline

The next morning my world came crashing down on me. The minute I opened my eyes, I remembered what had happened just twelve hours earlier. It hit me like a ton of bricks, a slap in the face, a punch in my gut. I could not stop myself from crying. Reality set in. I had no baby!

I dragged myself out of bed, went directly to the bathroom, and sat there, crying. "What do I do now?" My arms ached. My entire body ached. My womb was empty, yet there was no baby in my arms. I could not breathe, because I was sobbing so. Nancy heard me and was there in a flash. She stood next to me, her hand on my shoulder, feeling with me, quietly just being there. I told her that I wanted to leave to go see my daughter. I could not contain myself; I wanted her in my arms, right then. She helped me get ready. As I searched in my overnight bag, I pulled out the T-shirt I had chosen to wear upon my return, knowing I would have my bundle of joy in my arms. My T-shirt was proudly labeled "BABY." I held it up to show her. She immediately fetched one of her own plain T-shirts and gave it me—a small gesture with big meaning.

As I showered and dressed, I kept replaying the entire labor in my mind. What had happened? This is impossible! From the time we heard the heart beating at 100 until the time the baby came out was one or two minutes. Why didn't she make it? It made no sense! Why? Why? I felt like I needed answers. Ken was being very quiet; I didn't know what to make of it. Did he blame me? What was he thinking? No matter what, I needed to go to her, right then. I could not leave fast enough.

Ken, my mother, and I left the birthing center, heading toward the hospital. We were all very quiet. What was there to say? I sat in the back seat because of my stitches, as it was the more comfortable one, and I stared at the empty infant car seat strapped in the seat next to me. My heart was breaking. I was crying a river of tears. As we finally arrived at the hospital to see Jacqueline, we made our way to the neonatal intensive care unit (NICU) floor. My first feeling was fear. I was afraid of seeing a baby, any baby. I walked with my head down, but my ears were fine-tuned. I could hear a pin drop. The soft, brand-new infant cries were like thunder, lightning, and a tornado—all in one.

There had been a nurse shift change, and the nurses on duty were not aware of our situation. We stood there in the hallway, telling the nurse that our baby girl had died the night before and that we wanted to see her. We had to explain that I had given birth at another location and that she had been transported to that hospital. A nurse then escorted us to a private room and politely asked us to wait. The nurse said she was going to get Jacqueline. She informed me, as kindly as possible, that Jacqueline was in the morgue and was refrigerated. She would be cold.

"I understand," I answered, very disappointed. It was very difficult to keep it together. Ken later told me that that was the very room he had sat in for hours the night before. I understood a little more why Ken had been so insistent on my coming. I imagined him sitting here alone, holding our daughter. All alone ... until Amy had arrived. Amy later told me that when she walked into the small room where Ken was waiting, he was sitting on the couch in a daze. She had hugged him. She did not want to say anything stupid like "everything happens for a reason." She actually does believe that but felt that saying it would just be some idiotic phrase someone uses to try to make you feel better even though that is impossible at that moment. It seems that Ken was cold, and since Amy herself is always cold, she had brought a sweater. It just happened to be a man's sweater, and it fit him. She gave it to him, and that little bit of comfort that she could offer made her feel better, she later told me. They talked and waited for me. I never arrived.

As we waited for the nurse to return, I continued to think of Ken sitting in that very room. The fifteen minutes we waited for her seemed like an eternity. She entered, pushing an infant cart. I slowly got up and made my way toward the cart. I felt that my baby was waiting for her "maman.", as I had chosen to be called when I first became a mother. My legs felt like there were ten-pound weights strapped onto them. I could not get there fast enough. It didn't take but two seconds. It was enough time for me to wonder, "What will she look like? What will she feel like?" I thought I had no expectations—until I saw her.

"Oh, my God! She looks just like Veronique!" I exclaimed. She had the same dark hair. Her hair would probably have turned blond just like Veronique's, I thought. "Does this one look like me?" I wondered. "Is this really my daughter? She looks like she is sleeping. Let me touch her." What disappointment I felt that very instant when I realized that she was, in fact, cold. How I regretted not getting myself over there the night before while she was still warm and so soft. "How do I snuggle with her now? Should I? Could I?" I knew this was my only chance. So I picked her up and held her close. I smelled her and lifted her pretty dress to look at her tummy. She was wearing a diaper! I was surprised to see that. I felt it was a barrier that I could not cross. I didn't think of looking for birthmarks at that moment. I played with her hair, thinking how sweet that it was the same as Veronique's. I looked at her fingers and toes and smiled. Veronique is the miniature version of her father. A carbon copy! The one and only feature that she gets from me are her toes. Jacqueline had the same toes as Veronique. She had followed in her footsteps.

The nurses had dressed her in a white dress with pink trim. There was a bow attached to her arm and a ribbon in her hair. She was beautiful! Gorgeous. I could not take my wet eyes off her. And I wasn't going to be bringing her home with me. My mind was like a record player that was skipping, constantly skipping, and all I heard was "You can't take her home. She's dead. You can't take her home. She's dead. You can't take her home. She's dead."

I laid her back in the cart and arranged her hands so they could touch, and I took out my camera. I got myself ready to take pictures. I knew I should. I just had to. I wanted to. I needed proof. "I did have a baby. Here are the pictures. She did exist!" I thought. I took a whole roll. I took a few with Ken holding her. I took shots from different angles and set my camera on different settings. I added the flash and then took it off. I turned the lights on and then took another shot with the lights off. I didn't want to take any chances. God knows why I didn't get a picture with myself holding my darling baby ...

I felt like we were in that room forever. What felt like an eternity was only forty minutes. The doctor who had cared for our baby the night before, the one who had worked so feverously to bring her back to life, came in to see us. I felt so close to him. I felt an intimate connection. This man had tried to save my daughter's life. I felt like I knew him. I could say anything to him. And this was our opportunity to ask questions. It would seem like I would have a million, but at that very moment, just a few came to mind.

"What happened? Why did she die? Don't babies survive all sorts of traumas—why not this?" But the burning question was "Would she have lived if I would have given birth in a hospital?" And, especially, "Would an emergency C-section have been performed?"

He calmly stated that, according to the medical notes provided by the birthing center, if I had been in that hospital, they would not have performed a C-section, because the labor was completely normal. By the time the heartbeat was at 100 beats per minute, we could see the head, when Nancy stretched the opening. A C-section would not have been advisable. He found no evidence of any wrongdoing on their part. He continued explaining that he had previously worked with that same group of midwives and had found them to be very competent. And that there was nothing to suggest any foul play. I felt a flood of relief as he spoke, even though I was still trying to get answers.

"We think your daughter may have Trisomy 21—in other words—Down syndrome. We feel like she has some features suggesting this," he added.

"What kind of features? She looks completely normal to me," I said.

"We feel that she seems to have webbed hands, which is a positive finding, indicating Trisomy 21. Also her facial features," he answered.

"What facial features? She looks perfect. Anyway, Down syndrome babies live all the time. Why did she die?" I asked, not wanting to get into a debate about my daughter's facial features.

"We don't know why. We took samples of her blood to do chromosome testing. These test results will be back in a few weeks. And I suggest you have an autopsy performed to get a much clearer picture," Dr. Wright said.

"Does this mean I had a stillborn baby?" I asked, my heart feeling very heavy.

"You had a live birth. Jacqueline's heart still showed signs of electrical activity when she arrived at the hospital, which tells us her heart was beating just moments before we started working on her," he said.

I almost didn't hear a word he said, because I was stuck on him saying my daughter's name. Jacqueline! She was real. Why couldn't she be with me? I wanted my baby. I wanted my baby with me forever. Why did she die? These thoughts crowded my mind as I sobbed openly. These questions would not stop repeating themselves. Knowing that she had been born alive helped me at that very moment, although I did not know why.

"I know you'll get home and think of questions to ask, so here's my card. Call me anytime. Even if it's months from now," Dr. Wright said. I took the card he handed me, wondering what else there was to talk about. Little did I know the endless questions that would crowd my every thought after I left the hospital.

I did, however, hang onto a sliver of hope. I wanted those blood test results and chromosome testing results back as soon as possible. Knowing that there was possibly something wrong with Jacqueline was, in a weird way, a welcome thought. Maybe, just maybe, it wasn't my fault. Maybe it was nobody's fault. Dr. Wright said we would be hearing from the pathologist shortly, as the autopsy we authorized was to be performed that very day. We would need to wait several weeks for the chromosome results.

Words of Wisdom

After the doctor left our private room, Ken and I sat together, staring at our baby. Tears were continuously flowing, and my mother, who had been there the whole time, was still quietly standing by. You could hear a pin drop. That's when the social worker entered. She knew exactly what to say.

"I'm so sorry for your loss. Can I help you with anything?" she asked.

"We have another child at home; she's three and a half, and she knows that we were having a baby yesterday. She's expecting us to return today with her sister. What do we say?" I shared this agonizing question with her, as Nancy had suggested.

"Tell her the truth," she responded.

"But we don't know why our baby died; what should I say to her when she asks me where her sister is?" I asked.

"Tell her you don't know why she died. And leave it at that. She's so young that that may be enough for her," she answered.

"What if she asks me if the baby was sick?" I asked.

"For a child her age, it's better not to say that her sister was sick, because she may associate sickness with death," she answered.

"Should I tell her that Jacqueline is in heaven with Jesus?" I asked.

"It's definitely a good idea to tell her that the baby is in heaven. Just be careful not to say that Jesus came to get the baby. She may be afraid that Jesus will come and take her away from you too," she answered.

"She was so looking forward to seeing what she called 'her baby.' I can't imagine her never seeing Jacqueline. We've decided to have a funeral. Should she come? Should she see her dead sister?" I asked.

"Yes, if you're able to make the experience light and without too much emotion, then let her see her sister. I would recommend doing so," she answered.

She handed me a few brochures on the death of children and how to overcome it. There was also a children's book on death—something about a rabbit mommy losing a sick baby rabbit. We stayed in our private room, looking at Jacqueline, a short time longer and eventually left, heading home, needing to be with our daughter, Veronique. I wanted her in my arms like I never had before.

3

Going Home Empty-handed

Telling Veronique

We got home before Veronique arrived back from Suzanne's house. When she saw us, she ran toward us and was simply happy to see her "maman" and daddy. She jumped on my lap and gave me a great big hug. I held her in my arms and teared up, fearing the inevitable. But she didn't immediately ask for the baby. A few minutes passed, and as she had been doing for months, she touched my stomach and gave it a poke. The difference was that her finger went down farther than before, as there was no baby to stop it. Some of you may identify with this, as I am one of those pregnant women who still looks very pregnant the day after delivery.

I then had a chilling thought. "Maybe I don't have to tell her. We can go on like this; she can think that the baby is still in there." That split second thought didn't last, as I am not one to procrastinate, not even in a difficult situation. I preferred to get it over with then and be done with it, no matter how excruciating it was going to be. So I took that opportunity to tell her that the baby was not in my stomach anymore. My eyes were spilling tears, and I was fighting as hard as I could to maintain my composure. She looked around.

"Where is the baby?" she asked.

"She's not here; she died," I answered. My three-year-old didn't fully understand my words at that point.

"Why?" she asked.

"We don't know why," I answered, thinking of the social worker at the hospital.

"Where is she? I want to see her!" she said, as she started crying. It turned into a major sob.

"She's in heaven with Jesus," I said, not knowing what else to say but thankful for at least being able to give an answer. She continued to sob, hugging me tightly. It lasted less than thirty seconds.

"Are you sad?" she asked, once she had stopped sobbing. It took everything I had not to break down, throw myself on the floor, and weep.

"I am very sad," I answered. My lips were trembling, and my eyes full of tears. She climbed off my knees and walked away. She returned with a tissue to wipe away my tears. Then she climbed back on my lap and hugged me. I was stunned at her reaction.

"I don't want you to be sad," Veronique said. Then she jumped off my knees again and proceeded to demonstrate how she had learned how to hop in one place and play hopscotch. And, for a while, that was the end of it.

"It's so easy for a child," I thought.

Thirty minutes later, Veronique came up to me. She seemed to want to ask me a question, but she hesitated.

"Why is my sister flying in the sky with Jesus?" she asked, with a questioning look on her sweet face. I smiled, unwillingly. This is still an ongoing question, and she continues to receive the same answer, over and over. We don't know why!

I must explain here the reason that Veronique said "flying in the sky with Jesus." I have made the decision to speak French to Veronique at all times, so when I told her that her sister was in heaven with Jesus, I used the word "Ciel." Where I come from, we used to refer to heaven as "Ciel," but the exact translation of "Ciel" is "sky." She translated our conversation literally. I must say that her translation made me smile.

After that dreaded day, I found myself having troubled thoughts like "What right do I have to be a parent? I was given a chance and couldn't keep my baby alive. Why should I be lucky or blessed enough to be allowed to keep the daughter I still have?" And, more importantly, I wondered, "Why on earth should I be given a second chance at having another baby?" I knew we had done nothing wrong, but these feelings and thoughts crept in anyway. I feel that, as parents, it is our utmost important duty in life to keep our children safe, and I had failed with Jacqueline.

The Poem

The days between her death and the funeral were a blur. The immense sadness I was feeling just could not be shaken. I felt dread. Everything was dark. I just could not imagine how life could ever be normal again. Anytime I thought of Jacqueline, I began to cry, thinking that all my dreams for my life, as well as for Ken's and Veronique's lives, would cease, our lives would never be normal again.

I did, however, find peace in sweeping my floors, so on any number of occasions, you could find me in the living room or kitchen, quietly sweeping my clean floors. Even the day I returned from the hospital, I picked up my broom. My mother said she would do the floors, but I insisted on doing them myself. The rhythm of the broom's movement, back and forth, back and forth, created calmness for me. And I constantly thought of the pink balloons I did not get. As I was one week late delivering Jacqueline, many people in my neighborhood and at the office had questioned me.

"You haven't had the baby yet?"

"You'll know when it happens, because there'll be balloons on the mailbox," I answered every time. I asked my mother to remember to buy pink balloons and joked that it would be funny if she had to get blue ones. I also asked my office staff to buy some to attach to the office door. Many patients were eagerly waiting to see our new baby, and they asked constantly about her arrival. I felt so sorry for myself that I did not get to have balloons on my mailbox. It is almost as if I transferred missing my baby to missing the balloons. I kept saying to myself, "I was supposed to get balloons. But there will be no balloons." I sat down and wrote what I was feeling and thinking. This is what came of it:

> Balloons on the Mailbox
> Balloons galore,
> Pink balloons because it's a girl,
> But there will be no balloons at the door,
> Because Jacqueline couldn't make it into the world …
> Instead, flowers grace our home,
> With well-meaning poems,
> From near and far,
> Thoughts and prayers
> Warm our hearts,
> And forever we will remember
> Jacqueline Olivia Hørup,
> Born June 3, 2004, and died June 3, 2004.

I don't think I will ever think of balloons the same way again.

Unwavering Support

When my pregnant friend, Amy, offered to help make the funeral arrangements, I didn't know what to say or how to thank her. How could I have even begun to think of funeral plans? She started out by driving to the funeral home. She picked out a beautiful white casket, just perfect for our baby. She arranged the little cards we handed to all the visitors and helped me find the perfect message to write on them. We chose "Footprints in the sand." She suggested that we print my "Balloons on the Mailbox" poem on the back of the cards, and I was pleased about that. She arranged the date for the funeral and the obituary for the paper.

I decided to have Jacqueline wear my baptism dress from thirty-five years ago. This dress had been worn by both my sister and me. When asked her opinion, my sister agreed that it would be fitting for it to be used in this way. Amy came by my house countless times during that time for various reasons. She picked up the beautiful baptism dress, newly washed and ironed by my mother, and took it to the funeral home for my angel to wear.

I asked Amy to pick a place for Jacqueline to be buried. She wanted to do anything and everything she could to help, as she told me that she felt so helpless otherwise. Amy later told me that she wondered how she could possibly pick the burial spot, because ultimately what she was really choosing was the spot where the entire Hørup family would be laid to rest. The responsibility of that decision was heavy on her shoulders, but it really helped me.

She met the undertaker and walked the entire cemetery, searching for the best place. Once she found it, she called me and told me she had found a spot under the oldest, biggest oak tree. Jacqueline would be sheltered forever after. We bought it, sight unseen, and purchased a beautiful black marble bench as her headstone. We chose "Now I lay me down to sleep, I pray thee lord my soul to keep" to be engraved on the bench.

Amy said that, at that point, it was all very businesslike for her. Making arrangements and doing tasks was very helpful for her, because it was the best way for her to deal with her feelings. She just wanted to help us cope with our enormous loss, and being able to arrange things for us made her feel like she was actually doing something to help. A friendship should never be put through such a test, but I am pleased and forever grateful for Amy's unwavering support during my time of need.

The Funeral

From the time we returned home from the hospital until the day of the funeral, I remained in my house. I did not want to do anything. I just wanted to lie in bed. And stay there. We started receiving many calls, and my mother was taking them all. The doorbell rang periodically, and flowers and food were being delivered. I remained in bed. My body was aching terribly. I felt like I had just run a marathon. I had pushed for two hours. I could barely turn around in bed. It was like I had done the most intense workout of my life. And I had nothing to show for it.

During this time, I did three things. I stared at the trees outside my bedroom window, I scrapbooked the pictures I had taken at the hospital, and I read anything I could lay my eyes on that pertained to losing a newborn. I really needed to connect with another grieving mother—someone who really understood me. I needed to read that she had gotten through her grief and that we could get through it too.

In one of the booklets, I read that we could bring whatever music we wanted to play to the funeral. I also read that the funeral personnel are comfortable with death and understand how parents have a need to nurture their offspring. They encourage having the parents present when getting the baby ready to be put in the casket. As the parents, we would be allowed to help diaper our baby, dress her for one last time, hold her, and rock her for one last time. I shared this with Ken, and we both agreed that we wanted to be with Jacqueline during those final moments.

The morning of the funeral, I woke up feeling both anticipation and insane excitement. I just wanted the day to be over with as soon as possible, yet I was also looking forward to it intensely. I was going to see my baby one more time. I was wondering if the embalmer had succeeded in restoring Jacqueline's newborn glow. I wanted to hold her, look at her body, and touch her.

Our family arrived at the funeral home thirty minutes before the doors opened to the public. The funeral attendant was welcoming but mostly quiet. I handed her a CD of soft French nursery music that I felt suited the mood. They escorted us to Jacqueline's casket and left us to have some private time with her. As we looked at her for the first time since the hospital visit, I felt intense disappointment. She did not appear as I had hoped. How could they restore her pink complexion five days after she died? What was I thinking?

"Pick her up," I told Ken. He looked at me and then sighed. As he picked her up, he realized that rigor mortis had in fact set in by then, and she was stiff. He turned to me and said so.

"Put her down. Put her down," I whispered. He then gently laid her back in her casket, and we spent the next few minutes just looking at her. We felt that we could not have our last cuddle without creating lasting negative memories too.

Francine had been occupying Veronique during this time, and when we were ready, we asked our daughter to join us. We decided to take the hospital social worker's advice and let Veronique see her baby sister. Ken picked Veronique up in his arms and brought her to the casket.

"Here's your sister," we said.

"That's not a baby," she answered, almost jokingly, and she reached down into the casket and poked Jacqueline's hand as if to prove it. She then wiggled her way out of his arms, running to the multitude of flowers, and was tempted to pick them to make her own bouquet. That was it for her. She spent the remainder of her time there running around playing, until my sister took her away.

I had asked my closest friends to meet me there fifteen minutes before the official starting time. I wanted their opinion as to whether or not I should keep the casket open. I felt it might just be too sad to have a small, beautiful white casket with the body of a tiny baby inside—no matter how pretty the gown was. My mind was made up though; I would keep the casket closed. I could not stand next to her for two hours, continuously looking at her. So I opened the casket for my very close friends and family to see. Up until then, I was keeping it together. Then Amy steered me away and handed me a small gift. I opened the box to find a mother-and-daughter matching bracelet set with Jacqueline's birthstone. She had purchased it that very morning. I attached Jacqueline's bracelet around her wrist, and I put mine on my wrist. There wasn't a dry eye in the room. I was having a hard time not breaking down and sobbing. I was very touched by Amy's gift. I could not stop myself from crying; Amy could not either.

Bel, having her own struggles with this day, was the designated photographer. She tried to maintain her composure while taking the pictures, but I could see her struggling. I was honored by her determination to remain calm and composed.

I had borrowed a beautiful wicker bassinet from my friend Keri to use during the first few months of Jacqueline's life. It was to be used on the main floor of our home for naps and such. It had been proudly displayed almost in the center of my living room, ready to receive its bundle of joy. Realizing that keeping this bassinet was a constant reminder of our loss, I wanted to return it to Keri. We decided to bring the bassinet to the funeral home to display some of the many flowers we had received. It made a bittersweet prop, but it was beautiful.

Another prop we decided to take to the funeral home was a beautiful hand-painted painting that had been made especially for Jacqueline by my friend Cathy. It was a gift I had received at my baby shower. She had painted a teddy bear surrounded by blocks with letters that spelled JACQUELINE. It was beautifully framed and had been proudly displayed in the nursery. We decided to bring the painting to put next to Jacqueline's casket. When Cathy arrived at the funeral, I think she was shocked to see it there and started sobbing, stating that she had never painted anything like that before; she was almost apologizing for making it. I quickly told her that I cherished it because it helped to prove that Jacqueline had existed. I love it and always will.

So many thoughtful acts were performed by friends and acquaintances, and many stand out. Our neighbor Mike is the operations manager of our local beach patrol company. I had barely ever seen him in anything other than his beach "uniform." Never had I seen him before or since wearing a suit, but there he was, paying his respects in the middle of the day during his very busy season in June. He walked up to Ken and me, not knowing what to say. His presence spoke volumes. Over the next two hours, Ken and I stood next to our darling, accepting sympathy wishes from over two hundred people who came to pay their respects.

It is unbelievable what people will say when faced with an unfamiliar situation. Some people asked us why Jacqueline had died. One "friend" practically demanded an answer. Others were so awkward with their words that we ended up talking about the weather! Even worse, some talked about how their own children were doing. All I wanted was for them to move on so that I could sit down, stop talking, and take the game face off. I was in such pain. I could barely sit comfortably, and standing was excruciating. Everyone, meaning well, was hugging us, and my chest was so tender, because my milk had just come in. Those were the longest two hours in my life.

"Boy, she must have been some special baby! God just had to take her back right away," an acquaintance stated, smiling. I know she meant well, but I started crying all over again. Just when I thought I had regained my composure, Stacy arrived. She was pregnant with twins and experiencing a high-risk pregnancy. She had been put on bed rest during the twenty-fourth week of her pregnancy. In addition, she was still on very strict bed rest at the time of the funeral. She wanted to be there for me, so she decided to make her way to us. She was distraught and could barely walk down the aisle toward our tiny casket and us. As soon as I saw her, I started to tear up again because I was so touched that she had come. At thirty-three weeks, she was trying to hold off as long as possible before delivering her babies; as a result, she put herself at risk to pay her respects.

In the middle of the night after the funeral, Stacy began having contractions and was rushed to the hospital. She delivered her babies via emergency C-section at 12:20 PM. They were all fine. She had a healthy boy and girl. I could not get a word out when her husband called with the news, because I had been terrified for her. To this day, I watch her daughter and imagine mine standing next to her. They would have been one week apart in age. Would mine have been as tall? Would mine have started speaking, just like her daughter? Would I be putting Jacqueline's golden locks in mini ponytails too? Would her hair have been curly or straight? Stacy's child is my reminder—the one I compare mine to.

After the funeral, my family came with us to the Six Oaks Cemetery, where a few words were said by our pastor. I just wanted the day to be over with. I could not shed another tear. I was spent. My body had had enough, so we went home, where many of my friends had gathered. Suzanne had provided food for all of us, and we had a… what could I call it? Certainly not a celebration! Well, we got together for a few hours. It was a little awkward.

Bel had dropped off the roll of film taken at the funeral home to be developed in a one-hour photo developing shop. She brought over priceless photos of the baby, surrounded by beautiful flowers in her casket. We sat around the table, looking at the pictures. Bel had captured a fabulous picture of the beautiful bracelet around the baby's wrist—such a tender gesture and a heartfelt reminder of Amy's special gift. To this day, that picture hangs in the bedroom that was to be Jacqueline's.

The experience was surreal—sitting in my living room, going through the motions of making small talk with my friends on that day, with the many flowers and plants surrounding us. I have been told many times then and since, how strong everyone thought I had been during the funeral and afterward.

What is unknown by everyone is that I was on autopilot. Periodically, I felt awful, just wanting to crawl up the stairs and hide in my bed. At other times, I simply did not feel a thing. During these short periods, I was lucid enough to wonder why I was not breaking down. How could I be looking at pictures of my baby in a casket without continuously sobbing? Bel even commented later that she listened to me speak robotically, with details, about our experience during the baby's delivery. I had shown very little emotion. I think I can tell why I behaved this way. It was, perhaps, due to the powerful defense mechanism—the ability to detach—that I have built into my subconscious.

Defense Mechanism

I have always hated Sundays. When I was growing up, Sundays meant good-bye. It meant packing again. It meant having to leave my home, my parents, and my friends. It meant no more telephone or television. Because on Sunday, it was time to return to school.

The convent, St-Nom-Jesus-Marie, was set up as a boarding school, housing some forty students. It was located twenty miles from our home, in another small town on the outskirts of Montréal, Canada. This is where my parents thought it fit to send my sister, Francine, and I for structured academic teachings and religious training. Most kids were dropped off for the week on Monday mornings. My mother always dropped us off on Sundays. So, every Sunday, we packed our school uniforms and, immediately following dinner, we headed back to the convent.

According to my mother, she wanted to give us the best in life, had felt that we would receive a wonderful education there. For me, it was pure torture.

I hesitate in using the word "hate." After all, we are not supposed to hate, right? So I ask forgiveness for doing so, but I must say that I quite simply hated the convent. I didn't hate the religious instruction; I just despised living there. I felt that I did not fit in. Francine didn't either. It seems that we were set apart right from the start. It was as if we were foreigners. Maybe it was because our great aunt was a nun in the congregation. The nuns, afraid to show favoritism toward us, treated us with much indifference instead. They were cruel and resentful, to be more exact.

I was in fourth grade when I began attending the boarding school. All I wanted was to be home, with my friends, in my own room—not in a six-by-four-foot cell! That is what I called my living quarters there. The nuns referred to it as an alcove, separated by flimsy white curtains, acting like walls, from the other alcoves. It contained a chair, a nightstand, and a small, white, rod iron bed (like the ones we saw in war movie hospital scenes). I just hated the convent. I wanted to be home more than anything in the world. Not there, surrounded by people who couldn't care less about me. I was surrounded, yet I felt so incredibly alone, even though my sister was there too.

I begged and pleaded with my parents day after day, week after week, month after month, and year after year to spare me the agony of returning to that place. I lost my battle four years in a row. I prayed, as an eight-year-old would, for God to make my parents understand how I felt—how miserable I was.

This is where I learned to use my defense mechanism. It was innate. It kept me sane. Even though I continued to want to leave the school and go home, I began to care less and less, as I conditioned myself to not feel much of anything. I became hard and somewhat uncaring at times too. This defense mechanism has stayed with me my whole life. It is a self-preservation tool, at best. Unfortunately, this tool has also caused damage, as I can barely remember my childhood because I used it so much.

The only way I could deal with my feelings was to pretend not to have any. I did not understand my emotions, nor did I know what to do with them, because, as a child, I had learned that even though I felt bad, sad, confused, hurt, or mad, nobody would be there to reassure or console me, so I stuffed my feelings deep inside to prevent myself from hurting.

The most difficult period during my adolescent years was when my parents decided to separate. It did not take me by surprise, as there had been constant yelling and arguing in our home. I was actually relieved when it happened. Deciding which parent to remain with was what created chaos. I was incredibly mad at my mother for creating pain for my father, so my decision came easy. Francine was more concerned with loyalty; did it mean that she did not love our mother if she went with our father? She was torn. In essence, as children, neither of us should have had to make those adult decisions.

I chose to stay with my father, and Francine decided to stay with my mother. So sadly, my sister and I separated too. Moreover, as the final divorce was nearing, our parents were at war with each other, and we were the casualties. Francine chose to deal with the stress and pain of it all by numbing herself with drugs and alcohol. After years of destructive behavior, I am proud to say that she entered a 12-step program and continued on to make a full recovery.

My way of dealing with our terrible situation was to revert to old habits. My defense mechanism kicked in. I had perfected it, especially during my years in the convent. I was tough. Nothing could touch me. I blocked all unwanted feelings and hurtful memories. I managed to forget many things. And feel very little. My sister referred to me as "The Rock." I was misguidedly proud of this. Periodically, I crumbled. I broke down and sobbed, ironically, behind a huge rock in a nearby neighborhood park. It turned out that I was not the rock I thought I was.

I did not realize that I still had this ability to become numb. I know, without a doubt, that I unknowingly protected myself by going into a kind of trance in those early hours following Jacqueline's birth and in countless times thereafter. Unfortunately, my defense mechanism had a limit. Once reached, I began to feel. I felt the terrible grief of losing a child—along with many other emotions that I honestly would rather not have felt! Despair, doom, disaster …

4

Life Must Go On

Ken's Return to Work

The day after the funeral, Ken wanted to return to work. He felt like he could escape there. He was always very busy at work and could throw himself into it to forget, if only for the day, about his loss. He was very upset but was forced to constantly have his game face on. Being at work was ultimately what he wanted.

We had put a sign at the front desk in our clinic, asking the patients to refrain from asking Ken any personal questions. This may seem like an unnecessary request; however, chiropractors tend to develop long-standing relationships with their patients because return visits are frequently needed to enable recovery. In addition, I had been working in the office during my pregnancy, so the patients knew me as well. The patients felt connected to our family and would be grieving with us. Knowing this, Ken did not want to tell dozens and dozens of patients the same story over and over again. He could not do this and hope to perform his duties at the same time; that was just too much to expect. I had a short meeting with our staff members to give them some information, as I felt that they should have some answers. I told them they could ask me any question they wanted, and I gave them permission to answer any questions our patients may have.

We are like a family in our clinic, and I know that our staff and patients were really feeling our pain. What may seem almost unbelievable, though, is that some people wondered why Ken seemed so happy. They even asked! It was almost as if they wanted to see him cry. His style was to grieve silently, mostly hiding his grief actually. I understood then and still do now. In my opinion, men grieve differently in private too. I could not have asked for better support from my spouse, as he was always open to hear what I had to say and to cry with me, no matter how many times I needed to rehash our immediate past.

Thank-you Cards

I was feeling so empty inside, and I had so much extra time on my hands in those first few days and weeks. To keep myself busy, I kept a meticulous log of what people had done for us—the meals we received and the flowers that were sent. I had at least a hundred, if not more, thank-you cards to send. The thought of writing them all was painful, so I decided to have thank-you cards printed.

It was hard finding the right words to express our thanks. But what was much harder was entering the card shop to order them. As I entered, I immediately started crying and had to walk to the corner of the store so as not to make a scene. I piddled around as if I were shopping, trying to pull myself together. Once I felt I had myself under control I walked over to the saleswoman. I had typed up what I wanted to have printed on the cards, but when I tried to open my mouth to tell the saleswoman, I started to sob all over again. She looked at me, knowing neither what to say nor why I was standing before her in such pain. I simply handed her my note. I kept thinking that I should be ordering birth announcements instead ... earlier, I had leafed through the catalogs in this very store, wondering which ones I would choose, to announce the arrival of our newborn baby. Instead, I had to thank people for their thoughts and prayers for our angel in heaven. The saleswoman was wonderful. She quietly helped me choose the right ones for our occasion. I still see this woman from time to time, and I wonder if she remembers me ...

I kept all the notes we received. This note from the six-year-old child of one of Ken's patients stood out:

> **Dear Dr. Ken and Mrs. Ken,**
> **I'm sorry about your baby.**
> **Your baby is in heaven.**
> **We love you and care.**
> **You're still a mom.**
> **PS I'm sad too!!**

Putting Her Possessions Away

"A room fit for an angel." That is what was written on my favorite scrapbook embellishment that Keri gave me. I spent lots of time wondering what I should do with my angel's room. As a matter of fact, while still at the birthing center after delivering Jacqueline, I overheard my mother speaking to Nancy.

"What should we do with the nursery room? It is all ready and decorated," she had whispered sadly. I know she only wanted to do the right thing.

"Leave everything as is. Let Chantal do what she wants in her own good time," Nancy had instructed. Secretly, I was thinking the same thing, and when I heard Nancy's response, I was satisfied and agreed with the answer. I had been terrified for a moment that I would return to find an empty nursery, with all the carefully placed items packed away.

A day or so after Jacqueline's death, I was sitting at my desk, which is located between the nursery room and the laundry room. I had decided to write down all the details about Jacqueline's birth and subsequent death. I wanted to insert my story in her scrapbook so nothing would ever be forgotten. I spent endless hours working on these few pages, all the while thinking and feeling so low.

I noticed that my mother was silently walking back and forth between the nursery and the laundry area. She was washing the baby blankets, the bumper pad, the sheets, the changing table cover, and whatever she could get her hands on. She was lovingly folding all the items and neatly putting them away in the drawers and the linen closet. I was sure she was thinking that if it was all put away, and the nursery door was closed, then somehow I would not be reminded of my loss. However, my breasts were a constant reminder anyway. The milk had come in and had no outlet. I was suffering from empty arm syndrome. I felt that something was constantly missing. I could not forget even when I tried.

My mother often finds peace in performing various household chores, so I imagined that she just wanted to be useful and busy, especially in those first few days. Since Veronique was mostly taken care of by Francine or my friends, and there was not a baby to take care of, she may have been suffering from empty arm syndrome as well. Shortly after she was done with her "chores," I went behind her, opened the door, and proceeded to replace all the beautiful baby accessories back in their original places. I put the sheet back on the mattress and took the bumper pad and lovingly attached it with perfect bows to the crib railing. I returned the changing table cover back to its spot, and I sat in the nursing chair and looked around.

I could not imagine what I would do with Jacqueline's room, but I felt at peace when sitting in the nursing chair. I found peace looking at the decorated walls, even though it brought a fresh new well of tears to my eyes. I relived how difficult it had been to find the perfect matching crib skirt and sheet set—I had traveled to Atlanta, Georgia, to ultimately find it. I wanted it to be a specific shade of pink, and it just had to be a certain length. Unbelievable, how important that had been then. Also, I remembered how I had wanted a specific table for her reading lamp. What about all the clothes? Washed and ready to go. The newborn diapers were perfectly placed near the changing table. Diaper cream was on hand, ready to be used. Looking at all her things, I decided that I could not take them down or put them away. I felt that putting things away would mean the end of her existence in our home. I felt that I should grieve forever to honor her existence! I still could not believe what had happened. But my body constantly reminded me. I had just had a baby, yet I had no baby in my arms to prove it.

That is when I decided to find my camera and take more pictures to add to the scrapbook. I knew logically that I would eventually need to put things away. Not knowing at that moment if we would take the plunge and have another baby, I wondered if I should leave things intact for the next baby. Wouldn't it be morbid to use them again? What if I had a boy? I loved everything I had chosen so much that I could not change things yet, so I left the nursery intact for quite a while.

Autopsy Results

It felt like an eternity waiting on the autopsy results. My endless internal dialogue would not cease. What happened? Why did it happen? Finally, Dr. Wright called with the results. When I heard his voice, I knew this was the call I had been waiting for. Why did my baby die? It was my only question.

His answer hit me like a ton of bricks. He said there had been basically nothing wrong with her. She had been perfectly normal. There had been nothing wrong with her heart or her brain. I felt faint upon hearing these words.

"Why did she die then?" I asked, not listening to his answer, because I was consumed with thoughts of possible negligence or, worse, the possibility that her death had been my fault.

"There was an acute onset of the E. coli infection in the placenta. It had spread to the umbilical cord," he explained.

"E. coli? What do you mean E. coli? How did I get that?" I asked. There was no clear answer. When I heard "E. coli," I immediately thought of bad meat.

"Could it have been something I ate?" I asked. In the second it took him to answer me, I felt dizzy, thinking I may have unintentionally killed my baby.

He carefully reassured me that I had done nothing to cause the infection. The doctor said, "It's a fluke." I *love* that scientific term. Since then, I cannot hear that term without being reminded of Jacqueline. Dr. Wright continued by saying that the stress of the infection may have been too much for the baby's system to handle.

"Could we have known that I had that infection?" I adamantly asked. During my labor, I had not had a fever, which is an indicator of an infection. Besides the pain of the contractions, I had felt great. My temperature had been routinely taken three times during labor. I had not gone into preterm labor, which is another indicator of infection.

"The infection could have set in six, twelve, or twenty-four hours prior to her birth," the doctor said. It would have been impossible to detect or to have any reason to think that I had an E. coli infection at those times. I asked him if my "abnormal" stress test a few hours before the birth might have been an indication of infection.

"Could I have known then that the baby was in trouble?" I asked.

"No, because there was a strong heartbeat throughout the labor, and it is not unusual to have an abnormal stress test during labor. However, in light of the autopsy findings and the tests performed on the placenta, the abnormal stress test could have been an indication that something was wrong. But even if you had been in this hospital—a Level 3 hospital—with twenty doctors surrounding you, there would have been the same outcome, since there were no indications of a problem around the corner," he answered.

I asked again, "If I had a C-section, would it have been different?" He answered again that they would not have performed a C-section, no matter where I would have given birth, because the labor had been completely normal.

I will admit that this information was comforting to Ken and me, because until we received these results, we had thought, What if …? And could we have …? And did they …? Of course, there will always be "what ifs," but it was good to know that I could not have prevented her death—that it was nobody's fault.

Wouldn't it have been better to induce labor two days earlier? We will never know. It must be said that even the doctor could not say with 100 percent certainty that the infection was what killed her, as there was no sign whatsoever of the infection in the baby. He said to remember that sometimes babies just die. We will never know why. These words have since echoed in my mind.

A few weeks later the chromosome test results returned and revealed that Jacqueline did not have Trisomy 21 or, in other words, Down syndrome. I was surprised, since the doctor had put that idea in our heads immediately. However, I had never believed that she had Down syndrome, so that information did not hit me too hard when I first heard it. Within minutes though, I was intensely disappointed with those results. It seemed that it would have been better to have a definite reason for her death. Then I could have thought, "Maybe God took her to avoid any pain she may have endured." However, without a concrete reason, we are left guessing and wondering constantly, and the thoughts are excruciating.

My First Visit to Savannah

As Francine and I made our way to Savannah for my one-week checkup after delivering Jacqueline, so many thoughts crossed my mind. I was wondering how I would feel when returning to the birthing center. I know from experience that, on any visit there, I could find a new mother nursing her newborn in the waiting room. This is what originally attracted me to the birthing center. It was all natural. The midwives were mostly all mothers themselves, and there was no hiding in a corner to perform the most natural of duties—breastfeeding. This was one-stop shopping. Same location for your Pap smears, labor deliveries, and even your child's pediatric health care—all wrapped up in one. On more than one occasion, I visited the center with Veronique in tow, for both my checkup and her pediatric checkup too. While I was lying down with my feet in the stirrups, receiving my examination, Veronique would happily sit on my tummy, feeling as if she was on top of the world. She was never afraid of anything.

But how would it feel to come back after the birth? I was nervous about the reaction I may inadvertently have. Just one short week earlier, I had given birth to my beautiful angel, there, in that very location. She had lived there for a short time; she had been alive there. What a powerful thought that was. I was looking forward to showing the birthing room to my sister, feeling like I really needed her to connect with Jacqueline. I wanted her to understand how I had come to the decision to utilize that center, that group, those midwives.

As we entered, I instantly felt sadness. Actually, I was already feeling sadness, but it intensified. The staff members saw me and immediately called for a midwife to meet me at the entrance. As I expected, there were mothers, expectant mothers, toddlers, and newborns in the waiting room. Margaret whisked me away in a flash. She had been taking care of Veronique since she was a newborn. I felt comfortable seeing her again. After escorting us to the birthing area to have more privacy, we sat on the couch. I am sure that she was thinking of my well-being as well as that of the remaining patients in the waiting room. I agreed that those women did not need to hear me sob, nor did they need to learn of my situation.

"I'm so sorry for your loss, Chantal," she said, and the tears flowed. We talked for a while, and then she left us to see when Nancy would be ready to take me in. I showed Francine the room and relived my most painful moments. I showed her the actual bed I had delivered Jacqueline in and the tub I had been hoping to use again. I felt that the visit was therapeutic in many ways. A genuine feeling of peace came to me. Francine and I waited quietly, just being there, and when it was my turn to be seen by Nancy, I exited the birthing area and walked through the waiting room, looking at all the new life and expectant mothers. I know it's hard to believe, but it wasn't so bad. My internal defense mechanism kicked in again, and I kind of became a robot, going through the motions of walking through a tornado, trying not to be hit by flying debris, knowing that just on the other side of the waiting room door there was a safe haven.

Being face-to-face with Nancy was powerful. You see, there was only a handful of people who had had the opportunity to be in my daughter's presence while her tiny heart was still beating. Nancy is one of them. I felt sheer comfort in knowing that. She knew every detail of my daughter's existence. I also felt that Nancy held the answers to my many unanswered questions. Of course, I could remember none of them while sitting in the office. Thank goodness that Francine was there. She reminded me of what I constantly wondered aloud about. By then, we had received the autopsy results, and I wanted to discuss them further with Nancy. She was very patient in answering all my questions, and she thoughtfully asked how I was feeling and if I was planning on receiving counseling.

Unexpectedly, Nancy showed me her vulnerable side by stating that she had been over my case a thousand times and still could not figure out what had gone so wrong. In addition, based on her body language, I know she felt beyond awful about losing Jacqueline. I can't say that she felt responsible, but I'm sure she felt a certain degree of responsibility. I can't begin to imagine how she must have felt. I thanked her for attending the funeral with Jill and spending time talking with my family. My visit with Nancy gave me great comfort. My sister and I left the center, heading toward Memorial Hospital. I had decided to visit Stacy and her twins in the hospital. Francine agreed to come with me but made it clear, ever so gently, that she did not think it was a good idea to go see two newborn babies. I told her I wanted to go.

As I entered the hospital, I started feeling uneasy, but I felt a need to be there. Again, did I want to be close to where Jacqueline had lived, if for only a very short while? Or did I simply want to see a baby? I just did not know, but I soon found out, because, as I entered Stacy's room, I was relieved to find that her babies were not with her. She asked if I wanted to see them. How could I say no? On top of that, I am tough, right? The "Rock"—remember? I could handle seeing a couple of babies. I really thought I could do it, but as we made our way to the NICU, I realized that I just could not do it. I was about to walk through the very same door I had walked through a little over one week ago. That was when I had come to see my dead daughter. I stopped abruptly and told Stacy and her husband that I could not walk on. I immediately turned and walked away, down a very long hallway. Stacy later told me that she watched me walk away crying, as she stood outside those doors, and she cried as well. Francine and I left the hospital, quietly just being together.

Unfortunately, back at the hospital, Stacy was in a very difficult position. Because the hospital was full, they had kept her babies in the NICU until they were released, fourteen days later. She went inside the NICU every two and a half hours to nurse her babies. Stacy told me that she had watched many other parents go through the same ordeal that I was going through. She nursed her healthy, not quite five-pound babies, trying to hide behind the white screens they provided. She felt guilty that not only were her babies healthy ... but she had two! It seemed so unfair, she later told me.

She suffered from "survivor's guilt." Even to this day, she can feel it. The feelings have lessened tremendously over time. At the beginning, it broke her heart to see me look at her twins, especially her daughter. The first time I came over to see the babies, Stacy said it was heartbreaking. It was a moment that she will never forget. Apparently, I looked at them with such love and pain that it hurt her to watch. I honestly do not remember.

Stacy shared with me that she felt helpless. Seeing me was overwhelmingly sad for her. She told me that she never knew what to say or do. She did not know if she should cry, laugh, be quiet, or hide. Each time she saw me, she got nervous. Her internal dialogue went like this: "Should I say something about Jacqueline or not? Maybe she doesn't want me to bring it up? It might make her sad. Should I just not say anything? Does she want to see my children?" It drove her crazy, trying to say the correct thing and help me at the same time. She just did not know what was best for me. As time went on, her guilt sometimes increased, sometimes decreased.

The first three months after she had her babies were very exhausting for her. She told me that she remembers very clearly thinking, "Don't feel sorry for yourself. Your situation could be much worse. So get up now, and go feed a baby now! Chantal would give her right arm to feed Jacqueline." Knowing this gave her inner strength. She knew how lucky she was, and she told me repeatedly. With perseverance, she kept calling me. The more she was around me, and the more we talked about things, the better she felt. She realized that I did, in fact, want to talk about my baby. This actually helped us both to heal.

5

Remembering Does Help

My Outlet

Our family had moved into an awesome neighborhood four months before we lost Jacqueline. That is when I officially met Heather. She has since become an instrumental part of my healing. We live some five houses down from each other, but before I moved into the new neighborhood, Heather and I had seen each other around town occasionally. She tells me that she remembers meeting me at our daughters' gymnastics class several years ago. Apparently, as she sat in her sweat suit and baseball cap, I looked like I was ready to go to an evening out with my husband, as she put it. She later told me that she thought, "Wow, I really need to take better care of myself." We talked a little bit then and saw each other periodically afterward. We were, at best, very casual acquaintances.

When we officially met, we were both stay-at-home moms—the only ones in the neighborhood. It was only natural that we would start hanging out together, not to mention the fact that our daughters are the same age and play well together. In addition, we were just beginning to cultivate a friendship toward the end of my pregnancy. What is amazing about our friendship is that it grew mostly after Jacqueline's birth and death.

Heather had an innate sense of what I needed almost before I knew what I needed. She not only mentioned Jacqueline from time to time, but she also allowed me to talk about my baby without feeling that it was a forbidden subject. Her face was not tainted with pity, and she did not constantly wear her heart on her sleeve. Jacqueline was never a taboo subject. Whenever I felt low, and I needed to talk, she would drop everything and be there. Perhaps it was easy for me to share my feelings with her, because we had just become friends. She simply sat, listened, and asked me how I was really feeling. She told me to tell her anything—all the emotions that were being kept inside—and everything would always remain just between us. We spent hours crying, sharing, and sitting as our girls played together. Our daughters became inseparable. Heather was never afraid to ask me about Jacqueline, because she knew that talking about her was important to me.

Heather is a very spiritual person and is a self-proclaimed Christian-in-training. She has often said that my show of faith has since increased her own. Our conversations sometimes took us to why God did this, and wasn't I mad at God for doing it? In all honesty, I did not feel that way often. I accepted my fate—at some times better than others. When I was constantly looking for a reason for my loss, I sometimes thought that maybe I was destined to help concretize her faith.

Immediately after I got home from the hospital, Heather had organized dinners to be delivered to our door by neighbors and friends. We received a full meal every other day for one month. It was amazing how supportive people had been. Even strangers. I didn't know their names and had never seen some of these people before and yet they were delivering full baskets of food to my doorstep. Apparently, the rule was that they were to leave the meals there and not ring the bell. At first, when Heather informed me of her plan, I didn't think anything of it, but I soon decided that it was a great idea. Those first few days and weeks, I did not want to talk to anyone. I didn't even walk out of my driveway to get the mail from the mailbox for fear of running into someone.

On occasion, the "rule" wasn't followed, and people really wanted us to see that they cared. The outcome was a bunch of tears and much sobbing on both parts. I know everyone meant well, though.

A few days after my empty-handed return from the hospital, the phone had rung. I never answered the phone during that time. I had decided to glance at the caller ID and had seen that it was Heather.

"Hello," I answered. There was silence.

"Oh my gosh, Chantal, I didn't think you would answer. I was calling to see if I can do anything for you." I felt sorry for myself and was extremely sad, so I was about to start sobbing when she continued quickly.

"I'm so sorry for you; I'd like to do anything for you. Can I come over and paint your toes?" she said. And I laughed! This is exactly what I needed. Not the toenail painting but the laughing. This was just the first helpful act that Heather performed. It is ironic that Heather often mentioned that I should write a book about my experience. I constantly shooed away the thought, not putting any stock in what she said. Once I had, in fact, made the decision to take the plunge and write this book, I told Heather. She was thrilled and very supportive.

Veronique Looking Out the Window

Somehow, my three-and-a-half-year-old daughter, Veronique, knew when I was thinking of Jacqueline. Since I do most of my thinking when I'm driving, I inadvertently found myself daily in deep thought, constantly reliving that one day. I felt like I was stuck in one of those sci-fi movies where every morning when you wake up, it is always the same day as before. I guess my emotions were transparent, and my facial expression often betrayed me. Sometimes, Veronique would look at me in the rearview mirror while I was driving and ask me what I was thinking of. Other times, she would simply ask me if I was sad because of Jacqueline. No matter how many times she did this, it never ceased to stun me. She knew. How could this child know?

On one occasion, I looked at her and noticed that she had a pensive face, so I asked her what she was thinking of. I received the most shocking of answers. She kept her eyes on the sky and answered that she was thinking of her sister and that she really missed her. She would sometimes ask for an explanation, seemingly hoping that my answer would be different that time. It never was.

I am blessed that our tragedy didn't negatively mark or scar Veronique. We were always, and still are, very open about Jacqueline. I often read the book that the social worker at the hospital gave us, the one about the sick rabbit dying. Veronique mentioned once or twice that it reminded her of her sister. And, I always took the time to answer her same questions. Why? It was never a taboo subject in our home.

At first, since the sadness and pain of our loss was noticeable anyway, I often found myself admitting that I was, in fact, sad. Then, trying the change the mood in the house, we would sit at the kitchen table to draw together. She would draw her father, then herself, and then me. Sometimes Jackson, our deceased dog, would make it into the masterpiece. Other times, she added her imaginary cat. However, I felt there was something missing. I noticed that I constantly found myself wanting to add an angel to her family portraits. So one day I did, and she loved it. She then began doing it herself. This made me very happy and continues to do so.

6

Dare to Compare

Losing Ella

I was coming down the stairs on my way to the kitchen one morning when the doorbell rang and I found myself almost too close to the door to turn around and run. Therefore, I stood there and watched as my mother let in the parents of some friends of ours. They held a plant, intending to give it to me. There were tears in their eyes, and I knew they felt my pain. I was touched that they would come to offer their condolences.

"I know how you feel; it happened to me!" my friends' mother said. I was surprised and immediately teared up, feeling that finally I had found someone who could really understand what I was going through. Here was someone whom I could relate to.

"Really? You lost a newborn too?" I asked in a trembling voice, as I wiped my tears.

"I had a miscarriage," she said. I was stunned, to say the least. "That is not the same thing," I thought. "What are you talking about?" I struggled with these feelings for a long time after that visit. How can someone compare his or her loss to mine? At that very moment, my loss was worse than theirs, there was no doubt about that in my mind. At the very least, mine was definitely different. "Can one loss be worse than another?" I wondered to myself.

I really struggled with those feelings, especially with Bel. It took me a long time to finally comprehend that a loss is a loss, no matter if a baby is lost during a pregnancy or at birth.

Since I have moved many times, from country to country and from state to state, I have had the opportunity to meet many different people. I am an outgoing person and have had lots of friends throughout the years. Although many of my dear friends stand out, Bel is possibly one of my favorite friends. I feel it's kind of like the whole Oprah/Gail thing. Some of you may identify here. She and I have shared moments that only true friends can attest to. There is nothing I would not share with Bel. This is why I am still surprised that she was not the person I was the most comfortable to talk to about Jacqueline with. Maybe it was due to her loss. I never could have envisioned the pain that Bel had endured just six months earlier.

Bel is Cuban. She was born and raised, until the age of nine, in Cuba. Her parents wanted to give their children a better life, so in 1980 they prepared the necessary documents, hoping to leave Cuba for good. After waiting to be given the green light, they finally received their documents at midnight on Mother's Day. They had to leave with only the clothes on their back. In the middle of the night, by taxi and on foot, they made their way to the port, only stopping once to retrieve Bel's grandparents on the way. At dawn, they got on the boat, and by the end of the day, they arrived in Key West, Florida. They were then transferred by bus to catch a plane to Fort Chaffee, Arkansas. Once there, they were transported to a refugee camp, where they spent forty-five days waiting to be sent to their final destination, New Mexico. There, they started a new life. I'm always amazed that I actually know someone from my generation who has experienced this. I am thoroughly impressed with their courage!

Bel is one of those women who absolutely loved everything about being pregnant. She looked gorgeous at every stage. She never experienced morning sickness. She had a great appetite, and ate everything under the sun, not bothered with the typical immense weight gain. She knew she would simply shed her extra weight in good time. I believe that was what made her irresistible and charismatic during the pregnancy.

Her second pregnancy was no different from her first one. It was progressing beautifully, until the 23rd week. While standing in her kitchen, her water suddenly broke. After calling an ambulance, she was transported to the Hilton Head Hospital, where she spent many days under observation and intense testing. The diagnosis was that she had an "incompetent cervix," which was the underlying cause of the disaster. Lying with her feet, legs and pelvis elevated to keep the amniotic fluid from leaking out, she tried to maintain her pregnancy, although the risk of infection was great. In fact, her doctor advised her to terminate her pregnancy, stating that the risk was too great. Bel was heartbroken. She was forced to make a decision. Should she induce delivery, which was likely to be a death sentence for her unborn child? Or should she try to maintain her pregnancy and possibly develop an infection, which could create further damage to her, causing a possible deadly outcome? In the end, she delivered her tiny baby. And the baby didn't survive. This unexpected loss was shocking. Until then, there were never any problems. We were all flabbergasted.

The nurses at the hospital were wonderful to her. They dressed her little one-pound baby girl in a beautiful gown that Bel's mother had offered her for the upcoming baptism. They took a few Polaroid pictures. She was named Ella. Shortly after delivery, they took her away, leaving Bel lost and brokenhearted. How could she survive this?

I was sitting on my longtime hairdresser's chair when my cell phone rang. The news was devastating. I turned to Peg and told her that my girlfriend was having a miscarriage. Then I burst into tears. I was three months pregnant with Jacqueline when Bel lost Ella. I went to see Bel at the hospital and shared her grief with her, not knowing what to do or say. I tried to give the best advice I could, and to this day, I wonder if I was one of the people who said to her, "It's okay. You'll be able to have another baby." She was inconsolable. I know that I could have done and said so much more, if only I knew then what I know now.

Bel was released from the hospital on Thanksgiving Day. Our two families, as well as some of our extended family, had originally planned to host the Thanksgiving meal that year. I was making the turkey, and Bel was supposed to be making everything else. She and her family are fabulous cooks, and planning for a large group has never fazed her. The more the merrier. Rule number one is that there must always be an enormous amount of food, to ensure that we don't run out, God forbid! This is the Cuban family tradition.

When Bel got home from the hospital, it was decided that we would entertain as planned. And there she was, sitting on her stool, looking like nothing had happened, and we all took her cue and acted the same. The difference was that she was dying inside. She was so sad, struggling with her own feelings of guilt and shame, not to mention the aches and pains associated with birthing her baby just twelve hours before. Unfortunately, her family, like my own, thought that if we did not mention Ella, then Bel would get past it and move on faster.

What is amazing is that Bel had lost her sister some thirty years ago, just three days after Bel's sixth birthday. She remembers this vividly. They lived in Cuba at the time, and her sister, Karen, was six months old when she got sick. They found that she had a heart defect. After a risky, yet successful, operation was performed, it seemed that Karen had a chance of survival. However, due to a change in the nurses' shift, they moved Karen out of the intensive care unit, where she did not receive the care that she desperately needed. As a result, she died. Bel doesn't recall anyone in the family mentioning Karen after she passed away. She periodically asked her parents for some details but received few answers. She sensed that her parents categorically felt that if Karen was not mentioned, then life could resume normalcy.

Her parents are wonderful people, and they were by Bel's side as soon as her personal tragedy hit. They felt like they could help Bel move forward by keeping her focused on Lily, her first daughter, and her husband, instead of showing her that they too were mourning the loss of Ella just one day ago. This is one example of the taboo of speaking of the death of a child.

After what happened to Bel, I was devastated. I just could not think of anything worse than losing a pregnancy at her stage. And having to deliver the baby? What could be worse? The thought of expecting a baby, with everything going according to schedule, and then the baby passing away—it was the last thing I could imagine.

That Thanksgiving Day when our two families sat down at the dinner table, I looked at Bel. I sat in amazement, wondering how she could be sitting there with everyone. I was overwhelmed with admiration for her. The courage this took was unbelievable. I never thought I would someday be in her shoes.

I remember ten days or so after I lost Jacqueline, my sister and I decided to get out of the house. I didn't want to go anywhere; I was afraid, at that time, to run into anyone who may know me and ask questions. I didn't feel strong enough to answer without having a breakdown, so we decided to go get a pedicure some ten miles up the road. This is considered far from Hilton Head, because we live on a small island. We chose a place where I had never been before, thinking that I would be "safe." As soon as we entered, I ran into a patient from my husband's practice. She knew what had happened to me and was looking at me like I was a gorilla at the nail salon. She, with her mouth almost touching the ground, was staring at me without hiding it, not knowing what to say. I felt that I was reading her mind: "What is she doing here? Didn't she just have a baby that died? I can't believe she's out. She should be at home, mourning!" After more time passed, I realized that when she was staring at me, she was more likely to be thinking, "Wow, I can't believe she's out of her house. I'm so impressed with her courage!" I know she felt that way, because I felt this way about Bel.

Bel and Me

My scrapbook continued to give me great comfort. I found so much peace, sitting at my desk scrapbooking. I had never wanted my work to be as good as I did with those baby photos. None of my supplies seemed good enough. I felt that I didn't have the right paper or the right stickers. Nothing I had was good enough for those special photos. I shared these feelings with Keri and asked for her assistance. You see, Keri is my very own Martha Stewart. She makes her own cards and envelopes, no less. She can create almost anything with paper and scissors. When it comes to scrapbooking, she is a pro. In no time at all after our conversation, Keri knocked on my door. She had brought me a whole bag of different embellishments that she had purchased especially for me. I was touched by her gesture. Keri was also pregnant at this time and was using the same midwife group for her prenatal care. I know my loss had affected her a great deal.

I was ready to sit at my desk and pick up where I had left off with my scrapbook when Bel called. I started telling her about the new pictures I was about to work with. They were the pictures I took of the nursery, and I wanted to put them in Jacqueline's scrapbook. I explained that I had just completed scrapbooking the pictures taken at the hospital, and I wanted to share them with her. I'm not sure if she offered to come or if I asked her to. I just really wanted to show her the pictures of my baby again, so she willingly said she would come.

I realized at that very moment that I still had not seen a picture of Ella. Therefore, before we hung up the phone, I asked her to bring Ella's picture. I had asked once, after she lost Ella, and Bel had said that she would like to show them to me, but she never brought them. I didn't dare ask again, for fear that I would be reminding her of her loss. I never for one instant thought that she really wanted to share them with me, even though she had, in fact, once mentioned that she did. When I asked her to come see my pictures, I realized that maybe she felt the exact same way. Maybe she really wanted to share her pictures too. What was the harm in asking one more time?

When she arrived, we looked at our pictures with tears rolling down our faces. Neither one of us said much, but I felt that Bel wanted to tell me something. We had not had the opportunity to really talk at length yet. Alone, that is. Anytime she dropped by, there was always someone else there. Taking a deep breath, she told me that she could not imagine the pain I was going through, having completed the pregnancy, having had the opportunity to "know" my child for nine months, and then having it taken away. She stated that our situations were different. I thanked her for saying that, as I was thinking the same thing. But neither one of us elaborated further. I realize now, years later, that this was the start of our miscommunication.

Since I have decided to write my book, Bel and I have talked at length of our experiences. We found that we had one misunderstanding after another, which snowballed into us simply not discussing our feelings about our losses with one another. She has since told me that she had noticed that I confided in other friends more than I confided in her. This hurt her a great deal.

She also felt that she watched me from a distance. She wanted so badly to tell me that she needed me to confide in her and cry with her. She was my best friend and yet she felt that we were just ... friends. In our most vulnerable moments, we were not there for each other. Bel felt that I did not truly understand her loss. She knew I felt horrible for her experience, but she thought I did not equate mine with hers.

"Don't you know that I loved Ella more than life itself, that I am also grieving for a life full of cherished memories that will never unravel? How could you compare? Why would you do that?" she later said, sharing with me her deepest agony. Unfortunately, since we chose to talk of anything other than our losses, we really did not communicate accurately from the start. As a result, she felt that I compared our losses and felt that mine was worse than hers was. Nothing was further from the truth.

I must admit here that I did, however, feel that our losses were different. I continue to freely admit this. In the immediate aftermath of my loss, I could not identify with any other type of loss. I was alone, and there was no other loss that could compare to mine, I thought. I was not even able to identify with a mother who had experienced the loss of a stillborn baby. Not at that time, anyway. Since Bel and I did not spend much time talking about our feelings, we maintained our very good friendship, but I felt that I should not discuss my feelings with her. I did not want to remind her of her loss and dare to compare.

I also had a nagging feeling that she was mad at the fact that everyone was giving me lots of attention and mentioning how I had lost a *baby* but that everyone, including myself, was referring to her loss as a miscarriage. I clearly remember discussing my loss with an acquaintance, mentioning that Bel had also lost a pregnancy. Bel immediately interjected.

"I didn't lose a pregnancy; I lost a baby!" she stated forcefully. I was stunned to hear her say this. There was my best friend, to whom I feel the closest, and the one I care about with all my heart—and she felt this way. How could I not know? How could I, of all people, not be sensitive to this issue? Of course she lost a baby; why had I said pregnancy? Why did I think pregnancy? If I think this, doesn't the entire world probably think it as well? I started imagining Bel's internal struggle.

I knew more than anyone, except her husband and mother, I'm sure, how unbelievably sad she was about her loss. I have never before nor since seen such a happy pregnant woman as Bel had been. We all love our kids, unborn or born, but Bel was just beyond thrilled to be having another daughter. She wanted a sister for her daughter. She wanted Lily to have what she couldn't have—an unbreakable bond, a partner in crime, a best friend, a sister for life. I thought she knew that I understood—that I really got it. Bel and I had had conversations about our losses, but I was very sad that we had never really talked about our most private thoughts.

Ironically, only since I decided to write this book did we really start to talk at length about our feelings. It is such a shame that we let this need to compare our losses create such a riff. Thank God, we've talked about it since then, and our friendship is stronger as a result. Here there is a serious lesson to learn; even *a best friend cannot always read your mind.*

I realize now that I was not there for Bel, as I know I would be now. It took experiencing my loss to really understand hers. On the other hand, I felt that Bel, following in her parents' footsteps, was trying to *help* me to resume a normal life by not mentioning my loss. Ironic that, somehow, history finds a way to repeat itself. The fact is that no one, unless they have experienced it themselves, knows what to say to a grieving mother or father. Prior to my loss, I remember asking Bel how she was feeling one day.

"I'm okay today. But I'm worried about John. No one is asking him how he is doing," she said. The common thoughts were that "he's a man, he wasn't carrying the baby, he's just the father, he's fine, don't worry." However, people do not know that he was feeling extremely worried for his wife and was intensely grieving himself. I had not even thought of that!

I remembered this when Ken returned to work. It was as if from then on people assumed he was fine. But he wasn't. He was still grieving and really feeling our loss. He was scared of what our loss would mean to us, to our family, and to our remaining daughter. Would we have the courage to have another child? He wondered if I would be able to handle all the stress. He wondered if I would crack, fall apart? What would he do then? To my knowledge, not too many people asked Ken how he was feeling, except maybe Ricky, the grief counselor. For this reason, among others, grief counseling was very important for us.

The Drink

Our house has a detached garage. We built a mother-in-law suite over the garage to house the many guests we constantly invite. For many months after June 3, 2004, we continually had visitors. First, my mother and her fiancé Jerry came, then my sister with her family, then my father and stepmother, then my stepsister and her husband, then Marjorie, then more friends. Just when I thought everyone had come, it started all over again.

"Who's coming next?" Heather asked me.

"I'm not sure who's next on the 'let's not leave Chantal alone' campaign," I answered. Heather looked at me, stunned.

"Why? Should you not be left alone, Chantal?" she said.

I said, "Of course not."

"You're not thinking of ..." the words were never actually said, I believe.

But I quickly shook my head adamantly, meaning, "No way."

She seemed worried anyway. Honestly, the thought of harming myself never even occurred to me. I had Veronique to think of! However, I realized then that my family was worried about my well-being.

You see there is a serious history of alcoholism in my family, as well as in my extended family, and I have been told my whole life to watch out because "you never know when it will creep up on you." However, I have known for some time that alcoholism will not creep up on me. My first clue was when I was nineteen years old. I moved into my first apartment, and I felt grown up, even though I knew it was a temporary situation. I just loved hearing myself say, "I'm going back to my apartment after work." I did not even have to say it aloud; just thinking it made me smile. That is when I decided to celebrate being grown up.

I bought myself a bottle of vodka and a bottle of Kahlua. I was planning to make myself my first homemade "black Russian." I drank socially, and that was my drink of choice at the time. I carefully chose a crystal glass and found a measuring device to try to make the sophisticated drink correctly. I popped a Weight Watchers TV dinner into the microwave. Folded a napkin. Retrieved the remote control. I set myself up in front of the television, ready to enjoy my meal, with my fabulous drink in front of a *Three's Company* rerun.

"Now what? I eat and drink here alone?" I wondered aloud, as I looked around. I took one bite and then took a sip of my drink. Again, I looked around the room and thought, "How boring!"

"This is nuts. I don't want this drink. The only reason I made this drink is that I think this is what I'm supposed to do. This is not me," I categorically stated. Next, I proceeded to throw away the remainder of my drink and continued to enjoy my TV dinner. That was the first time I really knew that I did not have *the* "problem."

One day after Jacqueline died, I was having lunch in a restaurant with my sister.

"I don't know if I should have a Coke or a real drink," I jokingly said when it was time to order our drinks. The server suggested I try their house special, a margarita. My sister chimed in, saying that maybe a drink would relax me.

"It's only lunchtime. And I have been pregnant for so long that I have not had a drink in ten months. Who knows how that will affect me? So no thanks," I added. I did not think much of it at the time.

A few days later, at home after dinner, I decided to make myself a margarita. For social occasions, we have the necessary ingredients to make a mean margarita. My sister's words echoed in my brain. *It might relax me.* Why not?

I carefully pulled out the blender, trying not to bump into Ken as he was cleaning the dishes in the kitchen. I located the tequila, threw some ice in, and began mixing my "ray of sunshine." I poured it into a fancy glass and made my way to sit down in the screened porch, intent on sipping my "Rita." My eyes fell on Ken, and then, as if out of nowhere, my mother appeared. They circled me like lions, staring at me, not saying a word, but seemingly ready to pounce. They were watching me, almost wondering if I was, in fact, going to take a sip. I do not recall the exact word exchange between Ken and me, but needless to say, there was definitely no enjoying that drink. I realized in that exact instant that everyone in my household was just waiting to see me crack. They felt it was just a matter of time.

In my opinion, I felt I had already cracked, by breaking down and sobbing hysterically during the first few months, by not wanting to do anything with friends or have them around me as I used to, and especially by eventually letting my defense mechanism come down.

No matter how I felt, I decided not to give my family any more worries. *"Feeling better"* had to find another way in. I threw the whole margarita pitcher into the sink and walked away.

What is surprising is that, while discussing this book with Bel, she said to remember to mention what everyone was thinking.

"I don't know what everyone was thinking. How can I write about it? Do you know?" I asked.

She said, "I received many calls from your friends asking how you were doing and what could they do for you. Everyone was afraid you would not get over it!" she said. I was stunned to hear this. Apparently, my group of friends thought I would not leave my house for a year! I am just thankful that I did not know that then.

The fact is, if I did not "break" under *those* circumstances, then I feel that I am out of the woods when it comes to alcoholism.

7

Starting to Heal

Cemetery Visit

Unbelievably, I actually enjoy walking in the cemetery, looking at the names on the other headstones, looking at birthdays and the date of these strangers' last day on earth. I feel like I should get to know Jacqueline's neighbors. I enjoy seeing flowers on her grave. I enjoy seeing flowers on her neighbor's grave. I see how their loved ones bring flowers to remember their birthdays, and I assume some just bring flowers for other kinds of anniversaries. I feel good when I pick up fallen flowers and bouquets and replace them where they belong.

Looking at Jacqueline's burial site was difficult for me at first. Freshly churned dirt made its outline so visible. I could not wait until the grass grew over the site; then I would not be as aware that she was buried just below, in the sad white casket. When I returned so often to see her at first, I immediately looked to see if grass had grown.

Visiting the cemetery was therapeutic for me. When I mentioned to anyone that I was headed there, I always felt cold silence. For me, it was an opening—a way of saying "I want to talk about my baby." I usually felt that my announcement was received like "Oh, my God! She's thinking of her baby. Let me change the subject to help her think of something else." This just made me sadder. So I headed to the cemetery alone, feeling incredibly sorry for myself. I should add here that, over time, the only people who offered to come with me were Ken and Heather. How Heather knew that I needed to hear her offer, I will never know.

My friend Susan called to chat a few weeks after the burial. We had not had a chance to talk about what had happened firsthand. She had gotten tidbits of information through our mutual friends. She asked if I wanted to meet her. At the cemetery, she added. I was thankful for the location. We made a date and met—and she arrived armed! She had coffee for both of us and a blanket to sit on. She brought a journal and pen. I realized she had been there before …

Susan has two wonderful daughters from her second marriage, to Larry. She knows, without a shadow of a doubt, that she's been given a second chance at happiness. Some ten years ago, Susan was happily married to a great man; she called him her soul mate. One morning, he woke up, went to the bathroom, and simply dropped dead. He was not even forty years old! The autopsy revealed that his heart had skipped a beat and just didn't jump-start itself. Susan had been devastated. Not even thirty years old, and she was a widow. She had had to organize a funeral and choose a casket, as well as his final resting place. There had been so many things to take care of; I can't begin to mention them all. Steve was buried just a few rows away from Jacqueline.

Susan told me that she had spent a lot of time at Steve's burial site at the cemetery. She understood my need to be there in the same way with Jacqueline. She shared that writing in her journal was therapeutic and had saved her from herself on more than one occasion. This wasn't the first time I had heard this. I had also received journals from Bel and Heather. I was able to tell Susan my entire story, and she just listened. She teared up sometimes and laughed on cue. We talked about her loss too. There were no comparisons. It was a perfect morning. The taboo against speaking of the dead—an infant in this case—was nonexistent that day.

Some people may simply not understand the need that a mother has to be close to her child, even if the child is six feet under. It could be viewed as morbid, but nothing can be further from the truth. It's beautiful. We cannot nurture these infants; we can, however, wipe their headstones. We cannot groom our infants, but the surrounding plants can receive our attention. We are just being. Being there.

With time, I found myself busy with everyday activities, and I would skip a daily visit to the cemetery. Then another. I felt guilty, but I decided to throw that emotion to the wind. I knew I was right. I knew it and felt it. At one point, I hadn't visited her grave in a week, then two. Before long, it was monthly, then just periodically. No one told me to stop going there, even if it was thought. I stopped in my own good time.

People Who Do Not Know

Living in a small community, I was constantly running into acquaintances who did not know about our loss in the first few months.

"Where's the baby?" was a very common question. When I entered our local Barnes and Noble bookstore for the first time since the tragedy, the manager looked at me with a big smile.

"I see you've had the baby!" she practically yelled. I slowly walked up to her, trying to keep a straight face.

"Yes, but she didn't make it," I said. She was immediately horrified.

"I'm so sorry for asking," she said, as tears filled her eyes.

"Don't be sorry. You'll never get this answer again. It's a normal question," I said, trying to alleviate her horror. We both struggled to regain our composure as we walked our separate ways. Unbelievably, I later felt that when I would enter that store, everyone would look the other way. I didn't receive the usual direct eye contact. It could have been my imagination, of course. I just did not know how to react to that avoidance. I wanted people to mention Jacqueline. She was real—not in my imagination. I think about her all the time, whether she is mentioned or not. It is more upsetting to make believe that she did not exist!

The same kind of incident happened at our local pharmacy. The same woman had been working the cash register for years. In fact, when I first thought I was pregnant with Jacqueline, I bought a home pregnancy test, and she was the first one to know, because she rang up my test.

"Are you hoping it's positive?" she asked.

"Yes," I had shyly answered. We had exchanged quiet smiling glances. The next time I shopped at the pharmacy, she looked at me, not trying to pry, I'm sure, but just wondering. I immediately shared with her that I was, in fact, pregnant. From that point on, she followed my pregnancy. Imagine her shock when I finally emerged from my house and entered the pharmacy for the first time since our loss. She could not have had a bigger smile on her face.

"Where's the baby?" she asked, looking around.

"She didn't make it; she died," I answered. At least I had had a few weeks to digest that information; the cashier looked like I had punched her in the face. I think that she decided right then to never again ask that question to any other customer.

And, when I returned to my local nail salon for the first time, I was dreading the questions. I naively hoped that because all my friends used that same salon, maybe one of them had mentioned our loss to the staff and they would not ask any questions. I must add that, after a while, I was open to talk about Jacqueline—almost to the extent that I was talking about her too much. But at first, I was too fragile. I would cry at the drop of a hat. I teared up continuously. I just did not want to make a scene like the one I had made at the nail salon some ten miles away, just ten days after our loss.

That day, the nail technician had casually wondered if I was from around there. I answered yes. I told him that I usually went to the nail salon on Hilton Head Island, hoping the conversation would end there.

"Why you not go to there today?" he asked.

"Because I didn't want to answer questions about where my baby is, because my baby died, and I didn't want to have to say anything to anyone!" I blurted. I burst into tears, sobbing openly. I thought that everyone had been looking at me, but I have no idea if I was right because I had buried my face in my hands. The poor nail technician said something in Korean to his co-worker and didn't utter a word to me for the remainder of my pedicure.

At my regular salon, they were not, as I had dared to hope, aware of my loss, but when they asked how my new baby was, I was still much better equipped to answer. I did not break down, and to my surprise, that was the first time that I really wanted to explain what had happened. I tried to explain it in plain English to my Korean nail technician. With a language barrier to overcome, I did as best I could. He said he was sorry, and that was it! I was on the road to recovery.

Offering Her Possessions as Gifts

Like many expectant mothers, I had found myself window-shopping for baby clothes the day I found out I was pregnant with Jacqueline. I felt that I just had to have this and that for her. I continuously shopped for decorations for the nursery. On one of my shopping expeditions, I found a wood frame with a pink teddy bear tucked in a pocket entitled "angel." On another occasion, I found a giant "J" made out of gingham material. After she died, I just could not make myself give away any of the clothes and special decorations that I had bought. So I kept them. I purchased a small chest made out of mosaic china and neatly put all her leftover possessions in it. This chest is still, to this day, lovingly housed next to my bed.

I thought that one of two things would happen. I would become pregnant again and have another girl, and I would be able to use some of those adorable clothes, or I would slowly decide to pass them along. This is how Lucy, Marjorie's daughter, received a pink pantsuit and the pocket teddy frame originally purchased and reserved for Jacqueline.

I lived in Georgia for a little over five years while Ken attended Life University. My closest friend there is Marjorie. After attending my baby shower many years ago, finally the day came when I was to attend Marjorie's shower. I knew of her shower date at least a month in advance. Earlier, I had started knitting a blanket for her. It was pink and blue—my first attempt. My mother had knitted a blanket prior to Veronique's birth, and I felt that every baby should get a blanket as a gift. Unfortunately, Marjorie's mother had died unexpectedly when Marjorie was in her early twenties. I decided that I would knit a blanket for her baby in her mothers honor. Mostly, my critical eye could find a few small mistakes, but overall it wasn't so bad.

As I was ready to wrap Marjorie's gift, I opened my chest full of clothes and special memories of Jacqueline. I carefully chose one outfit that I had purchased. I stared at it. I thought, "Should I let it go?" It was a very difficult decision. Then I looked at the pocket teddy bear frame. "Should I let this go too?" "Angel" was written on it. Lucy was sent from God for Marjorie and David to love. Their Angel. I decided to give the frame and the outfit to Lucy.

Oh! How I had so carefully chosen this teddy bear frame to be placed in the nursery right next to the diapers.

I became very emotional, placing the gifts in a box, in tissue paper, as if it all could break.

When the day came, I drove to Atlanta to attend the shower. I eventually asked to be excused and took Marjorie aside. Wanting a private setting, we escaped into her bedroom, where I offered her my private gifts. I started crying before she had fully unwrapped the gifts. I could barely get the words out.

"This teddy frame was in Jacqueline's room, and this little outfit was an outfit I bought for Jacqueline," I sobbed. "It was on sale," I added. And we both laughed, remembering all those serious shopping days so long ago.

I found it therapeutic to offer some of Jacqueline's possessions as gifts to my friends' newborn children. Shortly after Bel lost Ella, her doctor gave her the go ahead to start trying to conceive another baby. Like me, Bel is blessed in that department. Her pregnancy was high risk, so the doctors instructed her to take many precautions to ensure a successful delivery. When her third daughter, Lola, was born, I gave her a pink, ruffled bathing suit and wrap that were given to me at my baby shower. It was a gift from Keri, who is a very close friend to both Bel and me. I was honored to see Lola wear it during the summer. The first time I saw Lola wear it, I felt a small, sad reminder for a fleeting second but then only happiness. I was looking forward to our trips to the beach, seeing her waddle all over in the beautiful suit that Jacqueline would have worn.

Then when I visited Stacy after she had her twins, I came with a small gift for each of her children. For her daughter, I chose another outfit that had been given to me for Jacqueline. It is hard to believe, but even though it was hard to give these gifts away, I felt really good about it afterward. Jacqueline was giving back.

The Letter

Imagine my surprise one day in September when I found a letter in my mailbox addressed to "Baby Girl Hørup." I stared at the letter, turned it over, and speculated as to what it was about. Who would call her "Baby Girl Hørup"? Who had before? The hospital. The autopsy report. The ER report. What could this letter be about? It seemed official. I opened it and found an invoice from a collection agency. They were requesting payment for the services provided on June 4, 2004—namely, the autopsy fee.

I had previously received our "explanation of benefits" forms from the insurance company for NICU services performed on the day they so feverishly tried to save her precious life. It seemed that we owed thousands and thousands of dollars. I called the insurance company to inform them that Jacqueline was to be covered under our policy. They asked why I had never informed the insurance company that I had delivered a baby. I then had to explain that my baby had died. I simply had not thought of calling them. They were very understanding on the phone, and I did not receive another form from them. They took care of everything.

However, for the autopsy, I had not received so much as a claim from the hospital, so I was unaware that there was an outstanding bill. Why should I be surprised to get one? Well, for one thing, the pathologist had mentioned that he was offering the autopsy as a courtesy, a free service, to us, seeing our pain and grief, I guess. I had no idea what an autopsy could cost, but I had just lost my baby, I was not thinking clearly. The pathologist had offered his sincere condolences at the same time.

I called the collection agency and made arrangements to send a check to clear the debt. I remember thinking that the agency probably thought I was making up my reason for not having paid for my bill. Good one, right! An autopsy for a baby …

An unexpected feeling came with that letter—almost a feeling of satisfaction. I was struggling with the memory of her life being erased. Gone! Like it had not even been real. The letter came at a low time. One would think that it would have been a reminder of my loss. I felt her loss on a daily basis; I didn't need a letter to remind me. For me, however, the letter was an acknowledgment of Jacqueline's life.

8

Helping Others

Christiana

Ken and I decided to return to our church shortly after Jacqueline passed away. I thought maybe it would help to be around people who had prayed for us. Until this time, my favorite part of the service was the singing worship both at the beginning of the service and at the end. Ken and I love this music and have chosen to listen to some great Christian rock music at home. However, what used to be so joyful to me was what almost kept me away from church.

I can say in all honesty that I am not angry with God for what had to happen in his "plan." But to sing "You have a friend in Jesus" and "How Great Is Our God" was just too much for me. I simply stood there with the others, except I was sobbing uncontrollably. I constantly and silently asked, "Why did it have to happen to me? Why us? I know she's with You, but I'd rather she be with me." The music allowed me to let a lot of my sadness and grief out. Every time I would start to feel the familiar, unstoppable sadness, I thought, "Okay, I'll cry this one time in church, and then I'll feel better." I found, however, that it happened more than just one time. I admit that I continued to go to church to see when I would stop feeling so sad. I was hoping Pastor Jeff's message would someday lift my intense sadness.

Then one Sunday, Pastor Joe took the stage. He had an announcement to make. One of the church band members Dean and his wife, Robin, just had a healthy baby boy. A picture of their newborn baby boy flashed across the screen. The feeling I experienced was a mixture of happiness and sadness at the same time. I was very happy for them, and I didn't feel so bad because they were showing us a picture of a baby dressed in blue. A boy. I felt rather detached because I had lost a girl. However, the other feelings of sadness were so powerful because I wondered why she had a baby that lived, when mine did not? What had I done differently? What had I done wrong? To top it off, their baby was born on June 1, 2005—almost one year to the day after Jacqueline. I'm sure that I was struggling with my own grief, as well as the timing of it all.

Living on Hilton Head Island is small-town living. This beautiful newborn's mother was Coach Robin from my daughter Veronique's gymnastics class, as well as a fellow church member. She had always been very sweet with the children at the gymnastics center, and I admired her talent. But that was the extent of our relationship.

A month later, while on a family outing at a local outdoor ice cream parlor, I ran into Robin. She was quietly listening to the lively entertainment while rocking her newborn in his car seat. The entertainer was none other than her husband, the same man who also plays his instruments at our church. I walked up to her and admired her bundle of joy, Kenneth. I sat down and chatted for a while about this and that. We were making small talk; I was asking if Kenneth was sleeping through the night and how the nursing was coming along. She asked such questions as how old Veronique was. I was not sure if she knew about Jacqueline, and I felt a need, as I did very often, to share it. So I told her briefly, without going into much detail. Like most people, she didn't know what to say, and shortly afterward, our conversation ended.

In an unbelievable twist of fate sometime in August, about one year later, I received a call after dinner. My friend Jennifer's voice was on the other end of the phone, and she didn't sound like herself. I waited a moment for her to tell me why she was calling.

"Do you know Robin and Dean from church?"

"Yes," I answered.

"I don't know if you knew that they were pregnant. She was induced today, and the baby died after delivery," she said, her voice trembling. I felt a punch in the stomach. I was dumbfounded! I didn't know what to say. I was so taken by surprise, as if my breath had been knocked out of me.

"Oh, my God!" was all I could muster. The very first thought I had was that I wanted to be with Robin. I wanted to leave everything immediately and go to the hospital.

"Do you think I should go? I don't know her well; maybe she has a lot of friends and family with her. What do you think?" I questioned Jennifer, hoping that she thought it was appropriate for me to go.

Unexpectedly, she said that she was hoping I would say that, because none of them knew what to do or what to say to Robin. As soon as I got off the phone with Jennifer, I walked into the bathroom and started sobbing. I knew the pain that Robin was going through at that very moment. I knew how she felt, and I felt it all over again—the desperation, the longing, the guilt, and the shame. The what-ifs ...

I had been entertaining Heather and her family for dinner that evening when Jennifer called. Upon my return into the dining room, Heather noticed that there was something not quite right. After receiving a short explanation, she offered to come with me to the hospital. Ken was out of town, conducting a continuing education seminar. Luckily, my family was visiting from Montréal. Through my tears, I tried to explain what had happened, asking them if they minded if I left immediately.

"Go," they said.

I remember that during the days after our loss, I was starving for information. I wanted to know if I was the only one this had happened to. I had looked for material to read—anything related to my loss. I had spent hours on the Internet. I thought maybe Robin would feel the same way. I had my story to give her, the one I was so persistently writing during those first few days and weeks. I printed it off and left for the hospital with Heather.

I was very quiet on the trip to the hospital, reliving my experience, just knowing, without any doubt, that I would help. I knew that, when I was in her situation, I had needed to know I was not alone. I must admit, though, that I did not think I was going to get to see her. She had had an emergency C-section, and I was sure that the nurses would stand guard at her door. Or maybe a group of friends and family would be there and that she would be too tired. To my surprise, as we arrived, a nurse was leaving her room. She looked at me with an inquisitive expression.

"I'm here to see Robin," I simply stated. The room the nurse was exiting from was Robin's room. She asked my name and poked her head back into the room.

"Chantal is here to see you," I heard her say.

"Let her in," Robin weakly responded.

As I walked in, there she was, in her bed, red eyed, clutching her tissue, with her husband at her side. My emotions got away from me, and the first thing I did was start sobbing, unable to get a word out.

"I'm so, so sorry for you. It happened to me too," I said, crying uncontrollably.

Once we regained our composure, I was introduced to her husband, Dean. I then told her what I had wanted to hear.

"I know it's rotten. I know this is the worst thing that could happen. It's unbelievable. I know, this is so awful," I just blurted out.

Then I thought, "Come on, Chantal, find good words. You can do better than that." But then I remembered, "Keep it simple, and say the truth."

"I'm so sorry for you," I repeated.

Since Robin's baby had been sent via medevac to a different hospital 150 miles away, immediately after delivery, Robin told me that she had not had a chance to see, hold, or feel her daughter, Christiana. The doctors had worked on the baby feverishly, but eventually the call had come that there was nothing more that could be done. Through tears and sheer pain, Robin had asked that the baby be baptized. Then the baby quietly passed away, with no family nearby. Robin and Dean were asked where they wanted to send the baby's body. Robin could not get a word out at that point. She shared with me that seeing Dean so distraught was a sight she had never envisioned. Robin and Dean were unable to make any decisions at that time, so our pastor, along with Al and Annie, very good friends of Robin and Dean, arranged to have the baby sent to a local funeral home.

Robin and Dean had made the decision to not see their darling little girl, afraid that it would create lasting terrible memories. Robin thought that seeing the baby would leave an ugly picture of death, as she put it.

"Do you want to see her?" I asked.

"I don't want to see her now because she may not look like a real baby. She'll be cold and maybe stiff; I don't want that memory forever," she sadly and honestly answered. After what I had experienced—seeing and holding my baby some twelve hours after she had been born and passed away—I knew her baby would still be perfect. Mine had not been stiff with rigor mortis after that time, and she had still felt very good, even though she was cold, so I knew that it would be okay to hold Christiana too. Careful to not overstep their boundaries, I explained that since Christiana had just passed away, in that last few hours, that she would still be soft and that Robin and Dean could cuddle with her, kiss her, and smell her. I told Robin that she absolutely must see her baby—that even though I had seen my daughter for forty minutes, I felt my time with her had been too short and that I had felt like I wanted more. It would never have been enough. What if I had never seen her? How would I have felt? As if God were standing next to me, helping me find the right words to say, I suddenly remembered a story about another acquaintance who had lost a baby. I felt a need to share this story with Robin.

Many years ago, while working at the front desk in Ken's chiropractic clinic, I met a woman by the name of Vicky. Her two children had accompanied her. For some reason, I asked her how many children she had, and her answer was that she had three. Her firstborn son was in heaven with Jesus, she had added.

I had immediately felt terrible. I know that I blushed and thought, "Good going, Chantal. You just could not mind your own business! You just had to remind her of her loss."

She saw my discomfort and quickly said, "It's okay. We don't mind talking about Tyler." I was astounded. Shocked, to be more exact. She proceeded to tell me that, on Thanksgiving of that year, she had not felt her baby move. Sensing that this was odd, she thought she would wait until the next morning and if there was still no movement she would call her doctor. When she did, her doctor told her to come in immediately. They searched for the heartbeat but could not find it. Tyler had died. She would have to deliver her beautiful baby boy, a stillborn baby. She told me that, once she delivered her baby, she took a few Polaroid pictures and held her little angel. She shared with me that she treasures these pictures and the short time she had with her son. I remember being amazed by her. How could she go on? That had been her first pregnancy, her first baby. What reason did she have to get up in the morning after that happened? I learned that she had the gift of faith. This had helped her tremendously.

When I first met Vicky, she had two other healthy children. What guts she must have had to try again and again. I was thoroughly impressed. At the time of writing this book, Vicky has had two more children, completing her family: four children with her and one angel spending eternity in heaven with Jesus. I told Robin this story, trying to help her see that, no matter what, she was better off seeing her baby.

Robin burst into tears, saying that she could not imagine spending eternity without at least seeing her baby girl once.

"Do you want to see your baby?" I asked, for the second time, gently looking at Robin.

"Yes," she said, nodding her head. Dean asked her if she was sure, and she cried, saying she just had to. Therefore, I left their room with a mission: I must reunite this family. I must reunite the mother to her infant. I felt that this was a matter of life and death. I requested that they send the baby back, maybe in an ambulance. The answer was no; arrangements had been made, and the baby was to be picked up the next day by the funeral home. I was told that the baby was in the morgue and would not, could not, be moved.

I just could not accept that. This was not right. Not possible. I walked over to Heather, who had been silently sitting by, praying.

"Heather, I want to go get that baby for her. Would you come with me?" I asked. Without a moment's hesitation, she said yes. This was a little out of the ordinary, but I knew that a parent could release the baby to whomever they chose.

The reason I knew that I could pick up the baby is because, when we lost our daughter, the nurse on duty at the hospital asked us if we wanted to bring Jacqueline home with us.

"Would you like to take her with you?" she offered. I had thought that my ears were playing tricks on me. I had thought, "Doesn't she know that my baby is dead? Doesn't she know who I am?"

"What do you mean?" I had asked, stunned.

"You can bring her to the funeral home yourself, if you would like," she had answered. I was taken aback. I thought, "Drive with my dead baby?" I just had not been thinking clearly. Ken and I had declined.

"What funeral home should we call to have her picked up?" was the nurse's next question. We had been standing in the hallway, discussing this with her, but I was on autopilot. Instead of calling my friends and family to come and see our beautiful newborn, instead of calling a photographer to take beautiful pictures of our newborn baby girl to send birth announcements out, I had to call a funeral home. Ken and I had felt lost. Tears would not stop rolling down my cheeks. Who keeps the phone number of the local funeral home handy? A phone directory could not be located. So I did the next best thing. I called Amy and asked her to look it up. As if on cue, she had asked if we would like her help in making the arrangements. That is when she took over and arranged what was necessary.

I knew that Christiana needed to be with her mother, and more importantly, her mother absolutely needed to see her, so I went back to Dean and Robin and asked for their permission to pick up their angel in Charleston. The proper papers were signed, authorization was given, and off we were. Heather and I left on our mission.

As we drove to Charleston, Heather and I talked about how I was feeling. Unexpectedly, I felt a mixture of excitement and anticipation. I was slightly afraid at what my reaction would be once I saw their little girl, but mostly I was excited at the prospect of reuniting Robin with Christiana. I actually thought Robin was "lucky" to have a chance to see her daughter. I longed for the same opportunity again.

In retrospect, I would have given anything for an extra hour with my baby, in the car driving from Savannah to Hilton Head on that fateful day. To have had her in my arms, smelling her sweet baby aroma, kissing each of her fingers, stroking her full head of hair. Maybe then I would have had the opportunity to scrutinize her tiny body, searching for any hidden birthmark. How I agonized over this after the burial of my baby girl. I started wondering if Jacqueline had a birthmark like Veronique. I played all sorts of scenarios as to how I would find out. Could I get the cemetery people to dig her up just for a minute? Just for one second … or could I do it myself? Would someone notice? These thoughts almost drove me crazy.

Once Heather and I arrived at the hospital, we were instructed to drive around to the morgue where the attendant was waiting. He silently and respectfully escorted us to where Christiana was. Heather must have asked me ten times if I was all right. I later found out that she was trying to prepare herself for what we were about to see. She then asked if she could say a prayer. We stood silently, with our heads bowed, for a few seconds. Then the morgue attendant pulled back the covers, and we finally saw her. She was so perfect—such a beautiful baby girl. I carefully placed her into the borrowed baby basket and covered her with lots of blankets to keep her warm. I strapped the basket securely in the back seat and signed the necessary forms, making sure I took our authorization paper. These stated that we were allowed to transport the "body." Then we drove off, heading back toward Hilton Head Island.

I kept willing the drive back from Charleston to go faster and faster. I couldn't wait to reach our final destination. Robin was probably waiting, eyeing the clock, or fitfully sleeping. I imagined her waking up every few minutes, wondering if the noises she heard in the hallway were possibly her angel coming to her. I remember the feeling of being squeezed and squeezed until I just couldn't stand it; I just had to see my daughter, and I couldn't wait a second longer to just lay my eyes on her. I felt it was my destiny to help ease that pain for someone else.

At one point, Heather and I had to stop for a bathroom break. We parked the car and sat there, looking at each other. Should we leave the baby in the car alone? Should we enter the gas station together? Everyone knows you do not leave a baby in the car alone. Did this rule apply in our case? We sat there, turned the car off, and wondered for a split second what to do. We decided that we couldn't leave her, so we took turns going to the bathroom.

At approximately 3 AM, we arrived back at the Hilton Head Island hospital. The only entrance open at this time of the night was the ER. The security guard was waiting for us. He quietly opened a side door and escorted us to the elevator. Once we arrived back at the maternity ward, the nurses were eagerly waiting for us. I delivered the baby to wonderful nurses who were ready and willing to make the family reunion a success. They dressed her in a pretty pink dress that Dean had chosen. A pretty hand-knitted pink cap was put on her head. Those fabulous nurses took so many thoughtful actions. They bundled her up and brought her to meet her mother. Heather and I left, feeling that Robin and Dean should share this experience privately.

The very next morning, bright and early, Robin called to thank me. Thanks were not necessary. I couldn't imagine not helping her. The thought never crossed my mind.

The nurses asked Robin if she wanted to be moved to another room, out of the maternity ward. There were not many births, but occasionally she could hear a newborn cry. She said no.

"I feel as if the staff and I had been through a war together. They know my case so well. I'm comfortable here. We'd all been shocked with the situation we found ourselves in. And they were all so kind," Robin later told me.

I knew that, on that day, the day after Christiana's death, Robin was probably feeling the pain of her loss in her soul, her gut, and her entire body, even worse than the day before. She had seen her baby, and then she knew that she would never see her again. She will never again feel the baby's soft skin or the touch of her fingers. It's so final. I remember those feelings only too well. As I drove away from my daughter that final day, I had felt such a terrible sense of finality. There is nothing to do. The grief is almost unbearable at that point, I remembered. There was nothing I could say to Robin, but I wondered what I could do for her. The only thing I continued to think of was that, when I was in her situation, I had wanted to find someone, anyone, who really knew how I felt. Therefore, I just wanted to be there with Robin, silently standing by her, in case she wanted to talk.

I then remembered that maybe she would not want to see me. I was a constant reminder to her of the day of her loss. What if she thought of me the way I did of Mary? My grief counselor, Richy, offered to put me in touch with Mary shortly after I started therapy. Mary had suffered a similar loss to my own. I was in fact happy to talk to her on the phone. I don't recall my thoughts at that time, but what I do remember is that sometime later, I met Mary in person in a social setting, and my immediate thought was sadness. Not only was I sad and reminded of my own loss, but I was also sad for her loss as well. We both live on a small island, so over the course of the first year, I often ran into her. I did not want to see her; she was a negative reminder for me. I thought that maybe I would become the same to Robin and Dean. I mentioned it to them, as lightly as I could. I wanted to give them an "out," in case they needed one. They both assured me that they didn't feel this way, and I proceeded to try to be of some comfort to them.

I was unsure if Robin and Dean had taken the time to read the notes I had left for them—my personal story. I was hoping that my story could shed some light on their situation. I wanted to help them know they were not alone. They mentioned that they read it, and after reading it, they both decided to give the go-ahead to have an autopsy performed on Christiana. They had originally declined, just not wanting to deal with it. They had been distraught then, and I fully remember just how difficult it was for us to make that type of decision under that type of stress. I know my story helped them to make their decision about having an autopsy performed too. The results gave them the answers they desperately needed. Christiana was diagnosed with Down syndrome with a fatal heart defect. Robin had opted not to have an amnio, so the baby's condition had not been detected. The outcome would have been the same either way, however.

There were several days between Christiana's death and her funeral. During this time, I received a few phone calls from friends and acquaintances who had heard of my involvement during Robin's tragedy.

"What can I do to help Robin and Dean?" was the question that was repeatedly asked. I answered as well as I could, making sure to mention that it was important to use their daughter's name in any conversation. I told their friends that it is much better to mention their loss than to not mention it, because ignoring the obvious is painful—much more so than reminding them of their loss. I also felt that it was important to help them remember their daughter; therefore, if a friend felt a need to give Robin a gift, then I suggested that a picture frame would probably be welcomed.

I understand that this may be difficult for most people to comprehend, but say, for example, that you have just given birth to your new baby and most of your friends, family, and co-workers come by in the days and weeks following. Everyone wants to see the new baby! Your friends do not usually come empty-handed. A little something wrapped in some beautiful pastel tissue paper magically appears, and the excitement of opening this gift is thrilling. When something so terrible goes wrong, and you are left without your priceless bundle of joy, then your arms are left empty. Visitors come with flowers and dishes of food. This is undoubtedly welcome. For me, when a little memento was offered, one that would last beyond the initial few weeks—it was very heartwarming.

Robin's good friend Holly offered a beautiful garment to dress her angel in. I offered Robin any assistance that she might need. Since my experience was unique, I could offer a viewpoint that no one else could. I had been there not so long ago. With this in mind, I asked Robin if she wanted me to take pictures of her daughter in her casket, as she had decided to keep the casket closed. This pleased her, so I arrived at the funeral home before the ceremony was to start. The funeral attendant escorted me to the casket. When I saw it, I was stunned! I was standing before the very same casket that Amy had chosen for my daughter's final resting place—a beautiful pearl-white mini casket. Unable to take my eyes off Christiana, as she seemed so peaceful, I began taking her picture with trembling hands. This time, I had a digital camera, so I was sure of my success. Remembering what Bel had done for me, I proceeded to go to a one-hour photo-developing shop and wait while the photos were being developed. I was anxious to return to Robin as soon as I could to hand her the precious pictures.

Since that day, I have remained very close to Robin, and we have formed our own little support group. At first, we met weekly to talk and work on Christiana's scrapbook. Once her book was completed, we continued to meet weekly and continued to scrapbook family pictures. I feel very comfortable talking with her about all my feelings, and I know she feels the same way.

After seeing a genetic counselor and following much soul searching, Robin and Dean decided to try to have another child, and I'm happy to report that Robin is pregnant at the time I am writing this book.

Another Loss

I was visiting with a friend, Gloria, when she informed me that her sister-in-law, Anna Maria, had had a baby seven days ago. She went on to say that the baby had passed away. Again, I was dumbfounded. I thought, "What's going on?"

Her case was a little different, as she knew that her baby would not survive for very long after the delivery. The baby had been diagnosed, a few months ago, with Trisomy 18 with a heart defect. The chances of survival are slim to none in these cases. Even though she knew her baby was going to die, she still hoped for a miracle. However, a few hours after the baby came in to this world, she left for a better one.

A baby dying is traumatic, no matter how it happens or whether you have had advance notice. I immediately called Robin and asked her if she wanted to join me in visiting Anna Maria. She jumped at the opportunity. I also called Bel. She was instantly willing to visit her, give support, and help with her healing. We knew we could be there for her as no other people could. We understood; we really understood. We had been there, so we could relate like no other.

I had met Anna Maria on a few prior occasions, as Veronique and I had attended her son Sebastian's birthday party. After her delivery, when we arrived at her home, I introduced both Robin and Bel.

During our visit with Anna Maria, we listened to her story and sympathized with her, and we cried and looked at her many beautiful pictures. She had started a scrapbook for her baby, Valeria. In her case, they knew that the baby would most probably pass away shortly after birth, so many preparations had been taken in advance. A new nonprofit organization in Savannah had been contacted. They provide the family with invaluable memories by offering to take professional photos of the baby as well as family members at no cost. These pictures were priceless.

She shared with us that her best friend was due to have her baby daughter soon. We all understood that this would be a very difficult time for her. I shared with her that when Bel went into labor with her third child, another daughter, I had known that I had to see her at the hospital, if only to at least offer my congratulations. I had entered her room with lots of courage, ready to brave the elements. I had held it together until her husband, John, proudly beamed at me, holding his beautiful newborn, all bundled up.

"Do you want to hold her?" he asked, just as proud as can be.

"No," I answered, bursting into tears. I was happy and thrilled for them, but I was intensely sad for myself. I felt so sorry for myself I just could not stand it. I stood at the window, looking out, sobbing. This was a very happy time for Bel and John—I simply could not enjoy it with them. So shortly after I arrived, I left. This was probably the second saddest day I had experienced since the loss of my own daughter. I felt gloomy all day long, struggling with feeling really sorry for myself and then feeling really guilty for feeling this way.

The next day, after visiting Bel and John, I decided that I was in control of my emotions and actions. I could choose how to feel, right there, right then. I made the decision to try to let the pain go and to enjoy Lola, Bel's newest daughter. As a result, sometimes I could not wait to see her, so I could hold her and feed her a bottle, but other times, I just did not feel that way. All in all, I feel that I dealt with my feelings to the best of my ability. Moreover, from that day on, seeing Lola just got better and easier.

9

Therapy Helps

A Vacation

I had had, in my opinion, a very difficult pregnancy with Jacqueline. I was afraid that I did not have the courage to go through another pregnancy. This was practically the first thought I had after Ken called to tell me that Jacqueline had not made it.

"I can't do this again," I had repeated over and over to Nancy.

"You don't have to think about that now," she had answered.

When I waddled around, working in Ken's office, many patients had jokingly asked, "Are you going to have another child after this one?"

"No way! I'm never doing this again, unless … no, I am definitely never having another baby!" I had said adamantly.

Repeatedly, I was haunted by those words for months after we lost Jacqueline. Why had I always felt the need to say that? Why had I said "unless …"? Even in those first few dark moments after Ken's call, I just knew that I needed to have another baby. I knew I needed it as much as I needed air to live. I would not be complete without one.

Ken and I were afraid of trying to have another child. What if the same result happened again? Apparently, the E. coli infection came out of nowhere. Worse yet, maybe she just died for no reason. Those words continuously echoed in my head: "Sometimes, babies just die." After a meeting with both our midwife and a genetic counselor, we decided to take the plunge, again. The chances of having another infection were slim to none. In addition, if it was not the infection that ended her life, then, it seemed, we had even better chances of a successful conclusion.

But would the next pregnancy be as bad? Would I be violently ill, as I had been with both Veronique and Jacqueline? I was terrified. What if it was something I had done that had caused our dreaded outcome? What if I caused it again? Did I want another baby enough to go through another pregnancy? Ken and I discussed it at length. I'm sure my questions were not always clear. I think I wanted a guarantee from Ken that this would not happen again, or possibly, I just wanted to hear him say repeatedly that it had not been my fault. As a result, Ken and I started having small disagreements, mostly due to the stress of our loss. Disagreements grew into arguments that scared both of us. We had heard stories of other couples whose marriages had not survived after the loss of their baby, so we immediately decided to not become one of those statistics.

We were told that we needed to start grief counseling. I wondered, "What is that? Grief counseling? They'll tell me how to grieve? What could be helped by that? Maybe they'll give us an explanation of the different stages of grief? I'll tell you what stage I'm in: I'm really mad! Why us? And leave me alone! Will they tell me how I can face anyone? And, especially, what if it happens again? What stage of grief is that? Grief counseling? Give me a break!"

However, Ken was adamant. He wanted to start therapy right away, so to appease him, I called and made an appointment as soon as possible. Of course, I thought that Ken needed to talk to someone, and he thought that I did.

Our first session shed a lot of light onto why we were feeling the way we were, and our counselor, Richy, gave us great tools for better communication. Our "grief counseling" quickly turned into couple's therapy! Any minuscule issue we had before June 3 had become an unbearable issue afterward. Not picking up his socks became a "make it or break it" problem. The smallest thing could set off a huge argument. We understand now that when we had an argument, it was usually due to being afraid of something. Richy asked on more than a few occasions, "What do you think he's afraid of, Chantal?" The answer was almost always right in front of me and made a lot of sense. We feared losing control, losing our existing child or losing our next possible newborn. Ken's fear was that I would not be able to handle our loss, causing our family to crumble.

I did need to deal with blame issues. I knew that losing our child was not my fault, and I knew that Ken did not blame me. What my mind did, however, was hear many of Ken's comments as possible accusations. The point is that, one year after we lost Jacqueline, I was still dealing with hidden guilt feelings. And Ken and I were too weak to handle even the smallest of arguments. For any couple with similar issues, I highly recommend the help of a third party.

A suggestion that Richy made as soon as we started therapy was to take time for ourselves, as a couple. She suggested that we take a vacation or start dancing lessons and also have a date night. Ken, again, adamantly wanted to take all her suggestions. So, off we were to take dancing lessons!

"You're so lucky your husband wants to take dancing lessons with you!" was a favorite comment among my friends.

I constantly thought, "I don't want to; he does!" So we continued the lessons, for a while, and it did start to be fun. Against my will, I enjoyed it.

Then we began thinking of her other suggestion to take a vacation—just the two of us. The last thing I wanted was to leave town and be unable to go to the cemetery. Or, more importantly, to lose control of my living daughter's every move. I became obsessed with "keeping her safe." I played the most unbelievable scenarios in my mind of how she could get hurt. My scenarios sometimes became extremely elaborate.

For example, I love long, leisurely bike rides on the shaded bike paths of Hilton Head Island. We can ride literally for hours and hours. During one of my trips, I imagined riding on my bike with my daughter strapped in the bike seat behind me, with her helmet securely strapped on. Suddenly, I hit a bump, sending my daughter—only her, mind you—over the embankment, spiraling down, all the way to the nearby ocean. I was paralyzed as I watched her go down under the water. My imagination was so vivid that I broke out in a sweat and had to stop the bike and push it for a while. I attempted to talk myself into thinking of something else as I tried to stop shaking. However, I was unable to do so. Against my will, I continued to play out that terrible scenario, seeing an ambulance arrive at the scene with medics who fetch her out of the water, then pronounce my daughter dead. I then saw myself going through the motions of being at her funeral and feeling so incredibly sad and heartbroken. Life was no longer worth living.

I imagined thinking, "Why go on? Now, both my daughters are gone. How can I possibly go on and, better yet, why?"

A horrible, real feeling of dread washed over me. "Why go on?" Right there, on the bike path, I wanted to die. Again, I tried to snap myself out of that morbid scenario but had great difficulty. Eventually and thankfully, my daughter, as if on cue, asked me a question.

"Are there mermaids in the water, Maman?" she asked.

And there it was. I began to think of something else. These thoughts hit me at unexpected times. Thankfully, they are fewer and fewer now.

But could I leave on a vacation? I wondered if I should leave my daughter. Ken was adamant about taking a vacation, so I asked my mother to come and babysit for us, so we could go on that vacation—the one we were told we really needed. The one that was inadvertently putting so much stress on me. I didn't want to go, but as I started planning it, I eventually got excited about it. Why not go back to the basics, back to the beginning, and find ourselves again? So we started to organize a fabulous trip abroad.

Second Guessing

Off we were. I was as ready as I would ever be, to leave my child behind and travel with my husband. Ken and I are a match made in heaven, especially when it comes to traveling. We change our minds unpredictably. We originally planned to go to England and Italy but added France and Denmark in the midst of our travel. We visited four countries in eleven days and returned home more exhausted than when we left. I must admit that the vacation was a very good time for Ken and me. We reconnected and enjoyed each other's company, and we especially laughed when we visited our old Pizza Hut restaurant in London. One server was still working there, thirteen years later!

Before we left on our trip, Ken and I had had much discussion and a consultation with our midwife, and we had decided to begin trying to get pregnant again. Therefore, we gave it the good old college try while traveling. We walked the streets of London, Paris, Copenhagen and Florence hand in hand during the day and worked on producing another child at night.

I really expected, based on past experience, to become pregnant the first time we attempted it again. I realize now that it was not the right time, because I did not get pregnant during our vacation. What was even more unbelievable is that, to my immense surprise, when we returned from our trip, I began second-guessing if I really wanted another child. I became terrified of having the same outcome, even though I knew, from the statistics, that that was very unlikely. Realistically, it was almost impossible for the same infection to set in again. I also kept telling myself that the doctors were never able to say with absolute 100 percent certainty that the infection had been the cause of her death. I replayed my conversation with the doctor who had cared for Jacqueline that night.

"Remember—sometimes babies just die," he had said. What guarantee did I have that my next baby wouldn't "just die"? I couldn't let my daughter, Veronique, witness my going through another difficult pregnancy if the outcome would be the same—not to mention putting myself and Ken through another pregnancy. So I started coming up with many reasons why I should not have another child. What if I was as sick as the last time? I may not have the same help this time. What if I could not get pregnant—for years to come? How long should I try? Then I started wondering if I really wanted another child. My mind was playing awful tricks on me, as I began wondering if I really had wanted Jacqueline in the first place. A terrible feeling of guilt followed these thoughts. "Did I make her death happen? Was it ultimately my fault? Had I not been pushing Jacqueline out hard enough? Did she stay in the birth canal too long and suffocate?"

I remember asking Ken, while I was struggling for breath between contractions, if I was pushing hard enough. His answer had been "You're not." I know he struggled with his own feelings of guilt that evening, as he thought the umbilical cord was wrapped around her neck. He thought that when he told me to push harder and I did, that somehow the cord got in the way of her entry into the world, causing her death. Poor Ken, sitting all alone in the hospital, holding Jacqueline, thinking that maybe he had caused her death. Thankfully, Dr. Wright had immediately put him at ease about that.

I still needed answers to my burning questions—especially if I wanted to have another baby. I felt that time was of the essence. So I dug out Dr. Wright's business card and thought about calling him. He had mentioned that I could call him anytime, if I had any question—any question whatsoever.

It was five months after June 3, sometime in November, when I decided to call him. I nervously dialed the number, not knowing if he would answer his direct line or if I would need to leave a message. What would I say? "Remember me, the one whose baby died?"

As I expected, the answering service picked up, and I left a detailed message, making sure to add our names, including Jacqueline's name and middle name and her date of birth. To my relief, he returned my call the very next day.

I was shopping in the mall when my cell phone rang. The caller ID listed a Savannah number. I knew it was Dr. Wright. I quickly found a quiet place and answered my cell phone. I had some provocative questions to ask. Dr. Wright was so patient with me. Even I realize that I asked him the same question four different ways, to see if a different answer would come. He was always willing to re-explore the same issues with me. I was very grateful.

There it was. My answer. The fact is that her death simply had not been my fault! It was official. I know the autopsy stated that too, but months after the results came in, I still wondered. In addition, she did not die because I was not pushing hard enough. She did not die because she was in the birth canal for too long. And it was not because I *did* push hard. Dr. Wright confirmed what I already knew—that the cord had not been wrapped around her neck. He reemphasized that my midwives did everything a Level 1 hospital would have done. It was nobody's fault. Even though I had asked him all of these questions before, I needed further endorsement to allow myself to start trying to produce another baby.

Ken and I discussed my conversation with the doctor at length, and the decision was made, once again, to try to conceive another child. I am truly blessed in this department, because, a few weeks later, I took a home pregnancy test, and it was positive.

"Here we go again. God, give me a break on this one. Please help me with the morning sickness and bless me with a healthy child," I prayed repeatedly from that point on.

10

Here We Go Again

Preparing for a Son

Although I was not working very much during my pregnancy with Jacqueline, I decided not to return to work at all after she passed away. I wanted to focus all my attention on Veronique. I wanted to go through every single moment with her. I felt as if every moment was possibly the last one. In addition, truthfully, I felt like a huge failure after we lost Jacqueline, and I could not face all our patients, day in day out. I did not want to see all their pitying glances—and worse—the way some acted like nothing had happened.

Therefore, throughout the nine long months of my third pregnancy, I was mostly at home with Veronique. That pregnancy was different from the other two. I had braced myself for the worst. I was amazed that I had almost no morning sickness at all. I felt nauseous on occasion, but I was not physically ill—not even once. It was a gift from God. I prayed about it, and I know many friends and family members put their prayer caps on for my sake, too, hoping I would be spared the terrible morning sickness this time around. I was truly amazed.

When the test results revealed that we were having a boy, I was almost shocked! A boy? "But I am supposed to have a girl," I thought. Veronique was supposed to have a sister here on earth. I saw myself shopping for two wedding gowns, not one. I was supposed to plan two weddings. What was I going to do with a boy? I had never visualized having a son. Shortly after the initial shock, though, I was thrilled. It is hard to believe, but I did get over the surprise quickly.

Heather asked me what I was going to do with the nursery after I learned that we were having a son. My first instinct was to do nothing. Why pour my heart and soul into redecorating the room? What if …? No. I would just remove the pink accessories and be done with it. Heather had other ideas, though.

Because of who I am, however, these "not decorating the room" or "leaving it to the last minute" decisions did not last long. Halfway through the pregnancy, I began casually glancing at some decorating magazines. I seemed to be on a lot of mailing lists, so I received many catalogs from various online stores. I found myself leafing through them, searching for a possible look for the room—the room I was not planning on redecorating. Then, one day, I saw a circus theme in one of the catalogs, and I was hooked.

Once again, Heather asked what I wanted to do with the room.

"I'm not sure," I answered. But I had a vintage *Dumbo* book and wondered out loud if the illustrations would look handsome when painted on the walls. I showed it to Heather, and she immediately visualized what would work in the room and how we could reuse most of the frames, shelves, and the lamp I already had.

Heather is without a doubt the most creative person I have ever met. Her friends, including me, are constantly asking her for decorating advice. We've told her on more than one occasion that she simply must start her own business. She is an accomplished artist and can turn any old piece of wood into a work of art; if you want it to look like an ancient Greek wall, you got it. And if it's art deco that you want, voila! Our local television channel has a home decorating show, and they have featured her house on the program. If she finds a pretty napkin in the sale bin at Target, she makes a beautiful pillow out of it.

Needless to say, I accepted her offer to help redo the baby's room. She asked for some chalk, stared at my *Dumbo* book for a few minutes, and simply started to draw on the walls. In a matter of minutes, she had laid out the outline for the animals, the tent, and all sorts of circus paraphernalia. I was in love with the idea.

I felt that familiar feeling of excitement in the pit of my stomach. For the first time during my third pregnancy, I saw myself nursing my newborn, sitting in the rocking chair and looking out the window. Then I looked over at the changing table and imagined myself changing a diaper. I even saw little booties in my mind's eye. And then, all of a sudden, my visual internal video came to a screeching halt. Was I crazy? What was I thinking? Why should I get excited about this baby? I could not be emotionally attached. I could not let my guard down; I might not have this baby to keep. Should I let myself hope? What if … I just could not stop my thoughts; they kept coming like an out of control train. I tried to stop the very dark thoughts that continued to creep back into my mind. Where was my faithful defense mechanism now? Death! That is what I saw. Just death.

Luckily, Heather, very absorbed in her creative burst, continued to move forward. I watched her work, choosing colors for the tent stripes. Turning toward me, she asked if I wanted to help. Temporarily, being involved in the decorating project made my morbid thoughts disappear.

"What will his name be?" Heather asked. I had a hard time answering that question, as I felt that if I picked out a name, then I would become emotionally attached from that point on.

"Tristan," I finally answered with a sigh. She proceeded to paint his name in a flag at the very top of the tent. It was official. She decided to get me even more involved with the painting aspect of the décor. She politely said that I was very good at painting her drawings.

"Yes, I'm good at painting inside the lines!" I answered. To this day, she maintains that I did a lot of the painting in the room, and I maintain that it would never have gotten done without her. Her creativity allowed me to keep many of the items I had purchased for Jacqueline. For example, the pink shelves were painted blue. I was glad that I had been able to do that. It was very therapeutic to work in Jacqueline's room while talking to her and praying to God. Before long, the room was alive and ready to receive its bundle of joy and finally carry out its purpose.

Honesty Comes from Children

One day, while I was pregnant with Tristan, the doorbell rang. I answered it, to find little six-year-old Olivia, a neighborhood child who lived three doors down. She silently handed me a note, turned around, and walked away. I love the innocent honesty that comes with most children. We can choose to help the new generation deal with the death of a child in an open manner. Her note made me smile, and I felt a warm feeling inside.

The note's message, written in a childish scribble, was this:

> **Dear Mrs. Shantel.**
> **What is your baby going to be a boy or a gril?**
> **I know you are having a baby because my mom**
> **and dad told me**
> **hope it will live because your last one deid.**
> **Good luck! Love Olivia**

11

As Times Goes By

One-year Anniversary

Imagine being at work, casually glancing at a nearby calendar, and noticing the date. All of a sudden, you mention to your co-worker that today marks the death of a very dear and close relative, maybe even your father. Your co-worker looks at you with an understanding look and puts his hand on your shoulder.

"How old was he when he died?" he asks. Then a comment like "he lived a good life" is passed, and no one is feeling bad about the conversation. If enough time has gone by since his passing, it is almost joyous to talk about it. You may even recall a nice memory and share it with your friend.

Unfortunately, unlike in this scene, any conversation about babies who have passed is not welcomed openly and, instead, promotes uncomfortable silence.

Most of my friends have understood with time that I would rather talk about my daughter Jacqueline than ignore her existence. Many of my friends, however, are uncomfortable bringing her name up. Maybe they are just trying to protect me, hoping to spare me further agony. I, myself, feel that way about bringing up Ella to Bel. I sometimes think that I may be reminding her of her loss in a negative way. How, then, can I expect my friends to understand? Heather, on the other hand, is the exception. She periodically mentions that she is thinking of my daughter, Jacqueline. I get a warm feeling inside when Jacqueline is mentioned. I realized that, if I felt that way, then maybe my friends who have lost babies would feel that way too. I try to mention their babies to them. It is hard, though. I know firsthand how important it is that our children are not forgotten.

Say, for example, that you have a child, and it is her birthday. You have decided to celebrate it by organizing a party. You carefully bake a cake and decorate it to the best of your ability. You buy decorations for the house and order balloons. You send out invitations that say, "We are having a party!" Everyone sings "Happy Birthday," as the children keep a watchful eye on the cake. You have a piñata filled with candy that the kids cannot wait to get their hands on. Then you watch your darling eagerly open her presents. The phone rings all day long with family members sending cheerful birthday wishes. Your child runs to the mailbox every day to see if another card has come, and when all is done, you send out thank-you cards. She is remembered, loved, and cherished. It can be seen and felt.

Then you have your other child's birthday. The baby who never was. She has a birthday too. Your very close friends and family members may remember. Do they remember the actual date? Should there be a celebration?

I feel as if most people are thinking like this: "Maybe I should not mention anything today. Chantal seems like she is doing so well. I don't want to remind her what day it is and hurt her feelings."

I am here to tell you that to *not* mention what you are thinking is worse than to mention it. What is not known to the general public is that we, the mothers, remember all the time, even though we may not mention it. How could I possibly mention my deceased daughter every time I think of her? Honestly, I often do not mention my feelings and thoughts simply because I am trying to spare the feelings of others. A feeling of uneasiness comes, sometimes, with some people when I mention Jacqueline. It is as if I had a contagious disease, and if we talk about it, then they or their families might be afflicted.

Jacqueline's birthday was fast approaching, and I wanted to celebrate my angel's day. A celebration may not be the correct term for what I felt was necessary, but a short remembrance ceremony was needed instead. I started thinking of what I could organize. A party? Of course not. Should I bring a cake? What was I thinking? I did not know what to do, so I decided to break the task of deciding what to do down into bite-sized portions.

First, I went shopping for invitations. I have always paid close attention to Veronique's birthday invitations. I had to find just the right ones for this occasion as well. After selecting the best cards, I printed out what I had carefully decided to write on them. I then sent them to my closest friends. Basically, I asked them to come, with their children, to the cemetery for a short remembrance ceremony. As I was thinking of what I wanted out of the day, I jotted down a few thoughts, and I ended up writing another poem. I added it to the back of the invitations. My only request was for my friends to bring a balloon. I called our pastor and asked him if he could join us at the cemetery to say a few words.

Hilton Head during the month of June is stiflingly hot, so I thought maybe I should bring a cooler with ice water. But how much time was I planning to be in the cemetery with my friends and their children? I was not going to make this a huge event. After all, it was not a party. I then admitted to myself that what was important to me was to have Jacqueline remembered. When my sister called to invite us to come to Florida and join her family in celebrating my niece Christina's birthday, I declined. (My daughter died on my niece's birthday, remember?) I just could not be with them. I wanted to be close to Jacqueline on the one-year anniversary of her birth and death. I needed to be home.

On the morning of June 3, I woke up, unsure of how I felt. Was I happy that the day had finally arrived? Did I just want to get it over with? Or was I looking for attention? For me or for Jacqueline? I was unsure.

I continued to update Jacqueline's scrapbook, and I knew that it was important to take pictures to create memories. I was hoping that they would eventually be positive memories. The scrapbooking was for me, but also I wanted Veronique, and any future child, to know his or her sister Jacqueline and how important she was to us. So I carefully packed my camera as I left my house.

I drove to a local party store to order a dozen pink balloons. I am sure that, when a bunch of pink balloons is purchased, there is usually some happy occasion to be celebrated. To ask what such an occasion is, is not a bad idea. Imagine the salesperson's face once he asked *the* question. I had been holding it together very well until then. I struggled to maintain my composure, trying to answer him before I started to break down. I told him that I was headed to the cemetery to honor my daughter's one-year anniversary. The look on his face was of sheer pain and horror. I felt just as bad for him as I did for myself at that very moment. I hurriedly exited the store and proceeded to have my first major breakdown of the day. It took me awhile to be able to drive to the cemetery.

All my close friends came, and most of them brought their children. I instructed everyone that, after the pastor spoke and a short, joyful reading from the Bible had been read, I wanted everyone to let their balloons go, to the heavens, to my angel. The kids really loved this part. They were running around as if we were at a park or something. I know that this helped me tremendously, and I felt that this was somewhat of a celebration of Jacqueline's short life. Each of my friends had gone out of her way to be there. Even a few of their husbands attended. We took beautiful pictures, especially of the children playing with Ken, and I still treasure them.

The poem I wrote on the invitation was this:

> "Balloons in the Sky"
> It's already been one year,
> How quickly time has passed.
> But my most powerful fear,
> Is the memory of your life won't last …
> You are always in my thoughts,
> And I carry you in my heart,
> My arms are constantly full of empty knots,
> Forever aching for a different start …
> Reach for the balloons flying in the sky, my precious baby girl,
> They are but a small symbol from our faraway world.
> June 3, 2004–June 3, 2004.

My Father

I have always been very close to my father, especially once my parents separated, as I lived with him during my formative teenage years. From the time I stopped going to boarding school until I left home for good, he was there for me at all times, and I learned many valuable lessons about leading an honest life from his example. Even after I moved away, I spent hours on the phone with my father, talking about everything that was going on in my life. He has always been very attentive, and I felt I could talk about anything with him. I really like him as a person. He is more than just my dad; he has always been my friend too. However, after Jacqueline's death, he never asked me how I was feeling and never brought her up either. I think that, especially during my father's lifetime, people just didn't discuss their deep emotions, especially those relating to the subject of a lost newborn. As I am not one to stay quiet, I decided that I wanted to try to talk to him about my feelings. He listened, and listened very well, I might add. To my surprise, he informed me that he had lost a sister when she was a baby. I was shocked to hear that.

She was the fourth child born to the Delisle family. My father was the ninth child, born about ten years later. He was never given detailed information about his sister, but he remembered hearing that his mother, my grandmother, had lost a baby. It was never discussed beyond that.

Of course, I was still starving for information about any infant death I could possibly relate to. Unfortunately, he had no details. He thought that the "little girl," as he put it, had recently started walking, when she wandered over to the water windmill saw and drowned. I asked her name, and he did not know. My first thought was "How could you not know your sister's name?" I could not politely, with any type of respect, say that to my father, so I asked him if he could get more details. He willingly stated that he would call one of his other sisters. One of them might have details or might have been alive when the tragedy happened. To my surprise, his sisters had very little information as well. They did, however, know her name: Therese Marie Delisle. They thought she had died of tuberculosis. The story was changing, and now, more than before, I needed answers. My aunts said they thought my eighty-six-year-old uncle, René, might have more details, since he had been alive then. I decided to pay him a visit myself. He was my favorite uncle on my father's side, and I looked forward to seeing him again.

This is what I found out. The baby, Therese, had been born with some sort of respiratory problem, and in the first few days of her life, she struggled to breathe and became blue on more than one occasion. Then, when she was approximately one week old, she turned blue again.

"She went blue and died," Uncle René simply stated. He shared with me that he was there when it happened and remembers his mother being completely distraught. When my grandfather returned from his workday at the railroad station, he found his wife holding their beautiful dead baby. He immediately left the house to buy a small white casket. When he returned, they proceeded to dress her in a pretty dress and lay her in it. The next day, they had a small viewing in their living room. Friends and family came. When the funeral was over, my grandfather and Uncle René went to a special area designated for infant burial and buried her themselves. Apparently, my grandfather was known for praying St. Therese throughout his life. My uncle said that it was a sad time, and I asked him if my grandmother had talked about Therese. He said that, at first, Therese was mentioned, but soon they stopped discussing her.

"After all, she was only one week old, and we really did not know her," he said. I do not fault my uncle for saying this, nor for thinking it. Most people, especially men from that generation, may feel the same way.

This was a telling tale about both my father's life and about how a baby's death has always been a taboo subject. My father and his sisters were not told how their sister died, as if not talking about it would help the memory to go away. Or maybe if people do not talk about it, then maybe it did not really happen at all. Life could then resume its normalcy. As if that is possible.

How sad for my grandmother. I imagine that, shortly after she lost her fourth child, she had to get up in the morning to make breakfast for her remaining kids while grieving silently. She went on to have many more kids. I can only think that her faith must have held her up. What is amazing is that I never knew this story, and I was only told because I had lost a baby. A telling part of this story is that my father has always said that he is one of nine children. The truth is that he is one of ten.

To this day, though, I wonder how my grandparents managed to produce so many children with no privacy whatsoever. They lived in a small two-bedroom apartment in Montréal. One bedroom was for the girls, and one bedroom was for the boys. My grandparents slept in a small alcove connected to the living room.

Their apartment did not have hot water, like many in those days. I remember my father telling me stories of his childhood, saying that, every Saturday, his mother would "clean" her kids. It took all morning for the stove to heat up enough water to fill up all the tubs and buckets needed. After that, everyone took turns taking baths, starting with the oldest son, going all the way down to the youngest child. My father remembers sneaking in one day after work and trying to take his brother's bucket. He did not get away with it. As a result, he had to wait until his brothers and sisters were all done.

I also heard that his parents were so poor that the kids got an orange and some nuts for Christmas. From what I gather, my grandmother bore one child after another in between cooking, cleaning, and caring for her family. My grandfather went to work at the railroad station every day of his life, never missing a day. They were poor, but happy.

In the early eighties, my grandmother simply lost consciousness due to high blood pressure one day and died in the hospital the next day. It was a shock for everyone since she had not been ill at all. The first time I saw my father cry was when he received the call that his mother had died. What a powerful memory this is—seeing and feeling my father's pain.

The second time I saw my father cry was just a few years after that. Where I grew up, there are parks on practically every corner. Although this was out of character for him, my father took my sister and me to a nearby park to break very painful news to us. My parents were going to divorce and were separating first. Again, the pain I saw in his face and heard through his words is a memory that has stayed with me.

The third time I witnessed his agony was when he felt mine. I know he would have done anything to take my pain from me. I know now, as an adult, the sacrifices he made for my sister and me. There seemed to be no limit to how much unhappiness my parents could take during their marriage to each other, until that day in the park when Francine and I heard the final words. He had finally reached his limit. When I spoke to my father for the first time after Jacqueline died, he just could not talk. Even though my sister had called my family in Montréal with the news already, I felt I wanted to speak to them myself as well. I was totally under control—at least my emotions were under control—until I heard my "daddy's" voice. From that point on, the pain was unbearable. His response was incomprehensible. The noises a human being can make during intense grief are indescribable. I am not comparing the three times I saw my father cry. I am merely stating that, in this third case, the bond between my father and myself was astonishing.

Reminders

Almost one of the first purchases I made, on one of the first outings I took after Jacqueline passed away, was a series of silver letters spelling out both Veronique and Jacqueline's names. Keri, forever the creative one and the pioneer among our lady's group, had gotten me involved in making my own jewelry. I decided to make a bracelet with their names. I carefully chose just the right pink beads and proceeded to make my bracelet. Then I remade my bracelet until I felt it was just right. I wore it around my wrist continually for months—actually, for probably a year, to be more accurate. I felt naked without it. And, truthfully, I really wanted people to notice it. It was another way for me to bring up the subject of Jacqueline. My friends knew I had made it and were respectful. I was honored when asked what the bracelet spelled.

"My children's names," I proudly answered. In many circumstances, a predictable question ensued.

"How many children do you have?" This brought up another predictable subject.

I had a very difficult time saying that I had only one child. That was a lie, and I felt that it tarnished and minimized Jacqueline's life. How could I forget her? How could I not mention her? She is my child, just as Veronique is. If I said, "I have two kids," then it opened up a completely new line of questions. I struggled with these feelings, as I was unsure if I was feeling that way for the right reasons. Did I want attention? Did I want to have my child remembered? In any case, I felt an intense need to mention her, especially when asked how many children I had. So I did. On some occasions, the conversation ended there, as those unsuspecting people just assumed that my other child was elsewhere. On other occasions, people asked how old my children were. I told them Veronique's age, followed by the mention of my newborn baby, who had died at birth and was "spending eternity in heaven with Jesus." My response was usually received like a powerful blow. Intense feelings of pity overwhelmed the person, as if they had somehow reminded me of my loss, and I sometimes found myself feeling sorry for them. No one is reminding me of my loss. I remember it always. I have just found a way to get past the pain.

Then there are the occasions when I simply cannot bring myself to answer truthfully, knowing that I am going to crush the person standing in front of me. On those occasions, I simply mouth silently, "Sorry, Jacqueline."

With every day, I have been getting stronger and stronger. My hope is that, someday, I will be able to answer these questions without hesitation—and feel good about my response.

I have always found peace while looking at the pictures of my angel. I had taken so many pictures at the hospital, but I was not using a digital camera and was unable to see if the shots had come out or not. I had thought, "Let me take a lot of pictures and hope for the best." Unfortunately, most of my pictures came out very dark. I wanted to have them touched up so that Jacqueline could regain her pink complexion. Where would I go? How would I do this? I imagined myself calling photo restoration companies, explaining what I ultimately wanted. I was uncomfortable doing this, especially so soon after her death. I found myself more apt to fall apart in front of strangers than in front of friends and family, so making these calls seemed unbearable. I mentioned this to my French friend, Aude.

Aude and I had met by total accident in our local mall. We bonded due to our common native language, French. She had just moved to our lovely island and was having difficulties adjusting from a New York City life, where she worked full time, to a low country, Southern life as a full-time mom. Periodically, we organized little playgroups for our children, to have the opportunity to spend time with each other and speak French. As it turned out, she had a part-time job working in a camera shop and was utilizing the "Photoshop" program on a daily basis. She willingly agreed to work on Jacqueline's pictures.

Aude later shared with me that it was very difficult to work on that picture. She digitally removed the discolored spots on Jacqueline's dead skin and replaced them with a rosy skin tone. Her second daughter was six months old then. She had to isolate herself to do this job, leaving her children to their dad in another room. She worked on the picture between nursing periods and at night, when everybody was asleep. She said that it was also very hard to have the picture developed. She wanted to be as discreet as possible, to prevent shock. When she called me to tell me that she had completed the restoration, I was beyond thankful. I really appreciated her attention and willingness to offer whatever help she could. I know that working on that photo was a difficult task for her.

I had received a beautiful picture frame as a gift, and it was just waiting to be used. It was proudly displayed on my dresser. We had countless pictures of Veronique decorating every wall in our house. I wanted to have a picture of Jacqueline in my bedroom as well. I asked Ken his opinion, and he said it made him sad, but that he was okay with it if I wanted to hang a picture of Jacqueline. I chose Aude's precious restored picture and inserted it into the frame. I stepped back and looked at it. Perfect. I realized that some people might not understand, especially since her coloring was still a bit off, making her look not quite right. But I did not care; she was my baby. When my sister entered my room and saw the picture for the first time, she gasped.

"Chantal, this is so sad. Are you sure you want to look at this all the time?" she said.

"What's the difference between looking at my albums or at this picture?" I answered. I tried to explain that having the picture close by made me feel better. She eventually understood.

Two years later, I found the courage to go to Savannah and enter a renowned business that specializes in photo restoration, where I had Jacqueline's original picture touched up professionally. I had it enlarged and framed it beautifully. It is placed on the wall in my office. I also made a shadow box. Attaching the giant gingham "J" I had bought for her bedroom door as a base, I decorated the shadow box beautifully, using many of the gifts I had received. I chose to add an outfit that my stepmother, Nicole, had given me at my baby shower. I had received a necklace from my sister, which I placed it around the neck of the mini silk hanger. I always loved headbands for infants, and Bel knew this, so she gave me a beautiful one that her grandmother had made. It is proudly displayed in the shadow box, along with a birth certificate holder containing her actual birth certificate. I added a card from the funeral home with my poem printed on it. Maureen had given me a mini teddy bear with a pearl necklace to honor her birthstone. This sits in the J. Right next to my shadow box and framed picture, I placed a sweet angel teddy bear that Maureen had handmade for us. This mini memorial, if that is what it can be called, makes me very happy. Jacqueline is remembered.

I cannot say that no one knows how to act when faced with our type of tragedy. I can say that there was just a handful of people in my network of acquaintances who did. Jill was one of them.

Jill, one of the midwives from the birthing center, sent my mother a letter shortly after that fateful day. The envelope contained a very sweet note with a copy of her banana bread recipe. She had renamed the banana bread "Jackie's bread" in our honor. She wrote that she would always remember Jacqueline, especially when baking her banana bread. My mother forwarded me the recipe, and I continue to proudly make it to this day. I was incredibly touched by this gesture. It means so much to me that someone, somewhere thinks of her.

A few days after the funeral, Ken and Jerry, my mother's fiancé, went to Home Depot to buy an arch. We wanted to install it in our yard and plant next to it two of the plants we had received. My father and stepmother bought a concrete birdbath, which we placed under the arch. I later made my own concrete stepping stones to add to my "memorial." I felt a need to have many items around the house as reminders. Another close friend of mine, Stacie, wrote a beautiful poem and attached it to a wind chime. We attached the chime to the arch, where I can sit on my porch and enjoy the sweet sounds and the view. I cannot tell you how many mornings I have woken up, made my way to the porch, and just sat there, staring at the arch.

Stacie's poem, attached to the wind chime, goes like this:

> Ring for me, Chime for me,
> As the breeze passes by.
> Chime for me, Sing for me,
> A Sweet Lullaby.
> Sing for me, Pray for me,
> My little heart can hear.
> Pray for me, Hope for me,
> Jacqueline forever dear.

Signs

While driving along our island's crowded roads, Ken had a minor car accident. He was fine, but there was a lot of damage to our van, even though the accident was not too serious. We decided to purchase another van anyway, to be safe. I have always had a habit of looking at other vehicles' license plate number and making words with the letters. At that time I continuously saw the same letters, JOH, my daughter's initials. Jacqueline Olivia Hørup. I saw them at least once a day. I realize now that I probably saw the same cars over and over again. Being on a small island, we end up driving past the same people often. Either way, I saw them everywhere.

While I was waiting for my new license plate to come in the mail, I was secretly hoping that those letters, JOH, would be on our new license plate. I felt that it would be a sign. My sign from above. How I hoped and prayed for it. When the license plate finally came, I was greatly disappointed. I mentioned it to Suzanne one day. I'm pretty sure I was near tears as I spoke.

"What do you think all those JOHs were? Don't you think those were signs?" she simply stated. I had not thought of that. Leave it to Suzanne to set the record straight.

JOH. Jacqueline Olivia Hørup. Remember how I chose Jacqueline's middle name? We chose Olivia so I could have my very own Jackie O. In another ironic twist of fate, I later found out that Jackie and JFK had also lost a child shortly after its birth in 1963. Their child, a boy, was born five weeks premature and lived for only thirty-nine hours. I should also mention that in 1956 the couple had a stillborn baby daughter. When I found this out, I felt a connection to her even more powerful than before. I wonder if I, on some subconscious level, knew that we had or would have something in common. I can only imagine how unbelievably difficult these losses were for Mrs. Kennedy. She was constantly in the limelight. Did she get help to deal with her losses? Millions of people knew she was pregnant and had lost her babies. Did anyone mention her children or did she have to mourn silently and pretend it did not happen?

For fear of not getting what I desperately wanted, I had never asked for a sign from Jacqueline until I read a book called *Don't Kiss Them Good-bye* by Allison Dubois, a famous medium. This book explained how we often receive messages from beyond, from our loved ones who have passed away. They contact us in any way they can reach us. Apparently, signs are often received in our dreams. I thought about it and thought about it hard. I casually asked Jacqueline for a sign—any way she wanted to send it. I asked casually, as to stay guarded and not get hurt, which has always been my MO.

This sounds like almost too much of a cliché to be believed, but I actually had a dream. In it, I saw my father's old construction truck. I clearly saw the advertising on the side door of the vehicle. There was a woman behind the wheel, driving. She was waving at me. And that was it. The next day, I was talking to my father and stepmother on the phone, when they mentioned that my father's deceased business partner's wife had just died, and that they had been to her funeral. I realized then that this was Jacqueline's way of contacting me, any way she could. The person waving from the vehicle was my father's partner's wife. This was the only way Jacqueline could connect with me at that very instant. I feel that Jacqueline saw her in heaven, and the rest was history. I know this is hard to understand, but let me just say that I felt peace from this dream. I look forward to seeing her in heaven. I have always known that she is there, but now I feel it in a different way.

Looking back on another event, I cringe at the thought of incorporating it within this chapter, as I do not believe in psychics. Clearly, it was not a sign. It is eerie, though.

While I was pregnant with Jacqueline, Bel had decided to throw me a baby shower; this one was to be a "Psychic Shower." Stacie opened her home for an evening of sisterhood fun. My girlfriends hired a psychic to give each of us a reading.

I have always been a skeptic, even though I love watching "Medium." I find myself really getting into the story line during the show.

Since I really did not put much stock in the validity of a psychic reading, when it was my turn to see the psychic, I had just one question for the woman. Was my labor with Jacqueline going to be easier than mine with Veronique? Throughout my pregnancy with Jacqueline, I had prayed that the labor would be faster and less painful. I knew what I was in for that time.

Her answer was particular, to say the least. First, she categorically said she saw three children. Everyone who knows me knows that I was going to have two children, and that was it. It was a well-known fact among my friends and probably most of my acquaintances that I was never going to undergo another pregnancy. My body just did not adapt well to "being with child." After hearing this information, I immediately was unsure of, and even more skeptical of, the psychic. I put no stock in her words from that point on. Next, she said she saw me with a baby boy in my arms. I knew I was having a girl. There was no mistake. My conclusion was that she was a fraud. Lastly, the answer to my original question was that the labor would in fact be faster and easier. She could not, or would not, go into any detail.

I walked out of the reading room, feeling like it was impossible for someone to accurately foretell the future! Why throw my money—or in this case, my friend's money—down the drain? My friends were eager to hear about my reading, and they had a great laugh when I told them that she saw me with three kids. Jokingly, we said that I might be having twins. Overall, we chalked up the experience to one great failure, hoping that maybe their readings would be better.

Why do I mention this? When I think back to this psychic reading, again keeping in mind that I am not one to seek out this type of information for anything other than pure entertainment, I recognize that the plan for my life was set in motion way before I was even pregnant—or alive, for that matter. I realize this not because of that psychic's information, of which I feel was mostly guessing, but simply because I know that God was there for me during my time of need. I feel I have proof of His existence, even though I did not really need proof.

Robin gave me a book to read called *90 Minutes in Heaven*. I started reading it while on a Thanksgiving cruise with my family. As I read it, the author, Don Piper, repeatedly mentioned that he wondered why God had let him die, then allowed him to see and experience the intense beauty of heaven, just to bring him back to a life of intense pain. Why just a glimpse? Why bring him back to major depression? He questioned continuously, why he had come back.

I found myself identifying with Piper. As I read his words, I heard the echo of my own mind—the continuous "why." Why did I have to go through my tragedy? What was the reason? Piper eventually got his answer and decided to write a book about it.

He wrote that it was his duty to share his information with the world. He was meant to help other.

Again, I identified. I feel that maybe I have gone through my ordeal to help others go through theirs. That maybe I am destined to tell the world that our babies should be remembered. This is ultimately what many mothers want. That a simple miscarriage is so much more to an expectant mother. That the grief felt by a mother of a twenty-four-week-old fetus is identical to the one of a mother of a newborn baby. I then had a powerful and scary thought. Am I supposed to write about it as Piper had? "I am not a writer," I thought. "I could get someone to help me, as Mr. Piper did. Can I do that? Really? Can I open myself up and show my vulnerability for the whole world to see?" I was consumed with these thoughts.

One day, as I was driving, I used my cell phone to call my sister, Francine. An avid reader, she often sends me books to read, and we periodically review these books together. What better person to discuss this with than her? I told her of the book I had just finished and explained my thoughts. By then, I had reached my destination, so I parked my car and listened to her response.

"Don't think of it as a book; just take it one page at a time. Think like you're writing a simple, one-page story," she said. As she was talking, I looked over to my right and saw a white truck parked next to me. I thought my eyes were playing tricks on me. The business name, clearly marked on the side of the truck was "Piper Plumbing." I was shocked! I had just finished telling my sister the name of the author, Don Piper. I know this sounds silly, but I really felt like it was a sign. My sign. I practically yelled it back at her.

A few weeks later, still pondering what to do, I met a writer by the name of Phyllis. This was a purely coincidental meeting. I was getting ready to have my head shampooed by Peg, my hair stylist.

"Does anyone know of a writer in the area?" I asked, thinking that if I did decide to "write" my book, then I needed to hire a writer.

"I do. My sister!" Peg answered, and she pointed to the chair on the opposite side. Phyllis was there. We spoke at length. She probably does not realize that she gave me the strength to have confidence in myself, and so I decided to write this book by myself. I can say, in all honesty, that that coincidental meeting is the reason I am writing this book.

12

Another Birth

Tristan's Delivery

The weeks prior to Tristan's birth were very difficult. Ken and I visited Richy, our grief counselor, many times during those weeks. I was very nervous about the upcoming labor. We both were. I felt that every word Ken uttered was some kind of direct stab at my ability to produce or deliver a healthy child. Ken, on the other hand, thought that I was taking every word he spoke too personally and that I seemed to misunderstand everything he said. He said I was "twisting and turning" what he said into something ugly. I should mention that Ken, who is Danish, only started learning English in 1990, and there are times, especially when faced with a stressful situation, when his words can be misinterpreted due to the language barrier. And, no doubt, I was sensitive to everything at that time as well.

During the pregnancy, I had a minor yeast infection. I mentioned it to Ken, and my recollection of his answer was "make sure you take care of that so we don't lose another child!" Needless to say, this became a huge blowout. We couldn't get to our therapist fast enough. When I relayed the story to Richy, Ken interrupted, stating that that was not at all what he had said.

"Am I crazy?" I thought. "Did I make this up? Surely not!"

Apparently, his recollection and mine were not at all the same. It doesn't matter what was said or who was right or wrong. We were both hurting.

"What do you think he's afraid of?" Richy asked. Mutually, our one and only fear was losing our next newborn. But we were not capable of discussing our disagreements and coming to some kind of understanding without the help of a professional. Once again, I highly recommend seeking the help of a third party in solving these types of crises.

As we got closer to my due date, I couldn't help but feel that my labor should be induced. Why take the chance of going past my due date and increasing the possibility of acquiring "The Infection"? I felt that I didn't want to take any chances. I had been told repeatedly that going past my due date last time was not the cause of my child's death, but why take any unnecessary chances?

My second worry was that, although I knew that it wasn't my fault that I hadn't been "pushing" Jacqueline out, I had pushed for two hours and had become really tired. I thought that I wasn't able to push her out in time because I might have lost my energy. I had been exhausted. I had pushed for so long. I was afraid that if that happened again, then maybe our precious baby would suffer the same consequences. I was afraid that I wouldn't have the energy to push if the birth took as long as the previous one. I was terrified! With my first and second labors, I had decided against taking an epidural. This time I was open to the possibility of taking an epidural. I was open to many different scenarios. The "all natural" route was out the window this time.

I knew that choosing to be induced meant a higher risk of having a C-section and possibly a 100 percent chance of opting for an epidural because of intense, immediate pain. Weighing all the risks, we finally decided to induce the labor one week early. We chose to deliver the child at a Level 3 hospital in Savannah. We chose a hospital where our midwife group had hospital privileges. These were all incredibly important decisions for us.

My midwife, Ken, and I discussed how we should proceed. We knew that a third delivery usually means quicker labor. We had decided that I would get a preventive antibiotic IV, just in case the infection was lurking and thinking of showing its ugly face. We were hoping to get at least two rounds of antibiotics in me before my water broke. These were precautions taken in case an infection set in. This is the main reason we wanted the birth to be induced.

Dreading *the* day, it finally arrived. I was to make my way to the hospital that evening, to be ready the next day, bright and early, for the Pitocin drip that would induce my labor. I woke up nervous. I did all sorts of household chores, knowing that I wanted to stay busy.

"Did we make the right decision? Should we mess with nature and be induced? Should I take the epidural?" I wondered aloud.

I called Amy to ask her opinion about inducing. I spoke to many of my friends, Bel included. I even called Nancy, again asking the same questions. Throughout my telephone conversations, I was nesting here and there and everywhere. I cleaned the floors, and to keep my mountain of questions company, I created a mountain of laundry to be done. I washed all the sheets, whether they needed it or not, and made all the beds. My mind was racing. By the end of my marathon, I was exhausted. I decided that I should lie down for a short while. It was 3:00 PM.

As soon as I put my legs on the bed, I felt a familiar cramp. My first contraction! "No, I'm just imagining this," I said to myself. It would be too great if I were in labor! "Lie down and relax," I thought. A few minutes later, I felt another contraction and then another and another. They kept coming. I felt a mixture of exhilaration and intense fear. "Great! I'm going into labor without being induced. No interferences. Thank God! Thank you. Thank you. Thank you. You are listening. Thank you for helping me,

Jacqueline." I thought this over and over. Then the fear came. "Oh, my God! I'm going into labor! I'm going to have this baby today. Quick, I have to go to the hospital immediately!"

I was already in labor, so I needed to get to the hospital fast to get the antibiotic IV rolling. I called Nancy, and as expected, she said she would be waiting. I was a pack of nerves. I called Heather so she could take Veronique, and I called Ken to tell him it was *time*. Before long, we were headed to Savannah. I was shaking with fear. I used my cell phone to call Bel at work, and her voice mail picked up. I began speaking clearly, but within seconds, I found myself sobbing on the phone, telling her we were on our way, and I was so scared. I cried most of the way to the hospital.

Our travel to Savannah was pretty quiet. Ken and I barely spoke. When we arrived at the hospital, we went directly to the maternity ward, where I was immediately started on the IV antibiotic. The contractions were five minutes apart. The time was 6:00 PM. The pain was totally bearable, but I was terrified that the contractions would intensify and that I would be exhausted to the point of being unable to push properly. I discussed my fears with Nancy again, and she reassured me, again, that if I wanted to take the epidural, then all I had to do was say the word. She suggested that we try a different drug first called Nubain. This drug was used to "take the edge off." She was concerned that I was going to be too afraid to push. Apparently, some women have that problem after the loss of an infant. I agreed to take the Nubain, because it was noninvasive to both the baby and to me. Nubain was designed to enter the system and "numb" the brain. It would be effective for a short time, but during that time, it would relieve all my anxieties. I was skeptical but very willing to try it if I needed it.

First, we got situated in our room. Nancy and Jill were with us, and I was being introduced to the nursing staff. I then noticed Gina and immediately felt an increase in my comfort level. The midwife who had delivered Veronique in 2000 at the birthing center was now the head nurse at that hospital, working that shift. She had been assigned to my room, along with my midwives. I found it oddly comforting that she was part of the team standing by to help deliver Tristan.

Eventually, the pain of the contractions became more intense, and it was obvious that I was not ready to start pushing. I was worried, so I asked for the Nubain. Moments after taking the drug, I had no more worries. I clearly understand how some people can become addicted to drugs. I had been incredibly terrified just minutes before taking it. After taking it, I did not have a care in the world. The contractions were still painful, and I definitely felt them, but my brain was focusing on counting the seconds throughout each contractions. Between contractions, I rested and found myself feeling nothing frightening or unhappy. My brain basically did not feel. I kept my eyes closed most of the time. Ken was on my one side and Nancy on the other. Nurses and midwives continuously walked in and out of my room. I heard them but did not care.

Nancy softly asked if I felt a need to push, and I shook my head no.

"Tell me if you do," she added.

I continued breathing and counting, then breathing louder, and counting faster. Eventually, I asked Nancy to check what progress I had made and how far I was dilated. I was in pain. I was beginning to be scared again. The magic drug was wearing off. I wondered, "Can I get another dose of that stuff? Should I take the epidural now? What should I do?" I asked Ken, but he was afraid to tell me what to do.

Nancy checked me and said I was fully effaced and dilated. She said I was probably going to need to push soon. There was no time for the epidural.

I was horrified! My worst fears had been realized. I was sure that I would be pushing for hours without help. I thought, "I'm going to have a hard time getting this baby out, too. I just know it. What if I can't do it? Oh, my God!" I panicked as these thoughts came rushing in within seconds after Nancy checked me. One second later, my water broke.

"Ladies, I think this baby may be coming soon…" I heard Nancy saying, but she did not have a chance to finish her sentence, because my body, without my knowledge, decided to *push*. All of a sudden, Tristan came flying out! Right into her waiting hands. There was a cheer, among surprised gasps, as no one had expected the baby at that time. Unbelievably, I cannot even say that I pushed. My body did, however. I felt like I had received a gift from God. Another one, that is. Not only had my labor been much easier, but I had also delivered a beautiful baby boy, screaming for all to hear. In addition, it was not even 9:00 PM.

Veronique Met Her Brother

The day after we delivered Tristan, I was very anxious to have Veronique join us. She had asked me on more than one occasion if she was going to be able to see "this baby." I always put on the strongest face I could muster with my reply.

"Of course you will. We'll be bringing him home, and he'll stay with us forever," I had said. Without fail, each time I answered her, I silently prayed that I was going to be right. Veronique was looking forward to seeing him so much that I had asked Heather to bring her over as soon as she could.

When Veronique entered the hospital room, her presence lit up the room. She was beaming from head to toe. I can honestly say that that was her happiest moment ever.

"I can't believe it. I just can't believe it," Veronique repeated over and over, while staring at him in her arms. We had place the baby on her lap with cushions and pillows all around him so Veronique's hands were free. She was holding her own head with one hand, nodding it back and forth, while lovingly stroking Tristan's head with her other hand. She stared at him, just in awe of seeing him, until she finally believed that we were bringing him home. Thankfully, he was indeed an easy baby to hold.

She had countless opportunities to cuddle with him and just look at him. She loves him so much.

I was dumbfounded when she asked me, a few days later, if we would be "keeping him." I understood then that she was still unsure what exactly had happened to Jacqueline. In time, she would get a much clearer picture. For then, I felt it necessary to simply answer that, yes, we would be "keeping him." Again, there is no trying to explain her happiness at that period of time.

God's Natural Drug

I know that Tristan's birth does not replace Jacqueline. I know this to be absolutely true. What I can say is that, since Tristan's birth, I am not the person I was before. By nature, I am not a depressed person, so I am not sure how much I can relate exactly. However, I have seen firsthand that, once a depressed person starts taking the proper medication, his or her life is forever altered. I feel like God provided me with what I like to call His "natural drug." My new baby. The second chance. The easier birth. The easier pregnancy. Prior to his birth, I was not walking around depressed all the time, but I was surely reminded of my loss in every daily task I did. I constantly felt empty-handed. Even when I was happy, out with my friends, shopping, or dancing, I was not really happy; I was not fully content. Even while I was pregnant, I dreaded his birth. I was constantly reliving that one day—the fateful day that I gave birth to my second daughter and, only moments later, lost her forever.

However, after Tristan's birth, there was an immediate change in me. I remember, a few days after his birth, I was at home in my room, nursing him, when Heather came in. I was talking about the labor, telling her how easy it had been, and I know I was very animated as I spoke.

"You want more children, don't you?" she cheerfully asked. Immediately prior to Tristan's birth, I had *always* thought, "That's it—no more pregnancies!" I must say I maintain this feeling now, but I can say now that I felt then like I could do it all over again, and again, and again. I know, without a shadow of a doubt, that I had help. Lots of help. I feel that I prayed for and received God's natural drug. His divine intervention. I know, too, that many people—friends and family members—held me in their prayers. There is no way that I am feeling this good just because I have a baby in my arms. There was in fact divine intervention. It is almost as if I can better understand "the plan," although it is still a mystery to me.

Maybe there *is* some sense to it. At the funeral, a friend said, "I know this doesn't make sense now, and you can't see the reason, but one day you'll know the reason. The thing is that when that day comes, you just won't care anymore." When that day comes, I will be with her ...

Another Birth

The day before I went into labor with Tristan, I decided to make a new bracelet. I purchased all the necessary letters to spell out Tristan's name and hired a professional costume jewelry artist to remake my bracelet using my previous letters and beads. Now my bracelet spelled out my three children's names. I brought it with me to the hospital, and as I was leaving with my new baby, I had my bracelet securely attached to my wrist. I was beyond proud to have birthed three children, and somehow, having only two of my children with me was acceptable. I wore my bracelet for months, until, one day, I just did not feel the need anymore. I guess I am comfortable with my life, as I feel I have less to prove now.

Bel tells me that she has also seen much change in me. She feels that I was always angry. She apparently got many comments from our friends that they wondered if I would ever get over it, being so angry all the time. I cannot say that I remember that. There is no doubt that I was angry. I was not trying to hide it. However, I also did not realize that it was that noticeable. When I really think about it now, I don't think it was anger that I was feeling. I think I was mostly sad and scared.

I do, however, remember when the tsunami hit after Christmas in 2004. I was not yet pregnant with Tristan. I had met up with a group of my girlfriends. We were casually talking of the disaster, and I let it be known that I felt terrible for all those lives that had been lost. No doubt that that tragedy was just not fair! But when I heard that they found a newborn baby floating on a mattress, all by itself, I was blown away by my feelings of anger. Why did that baby survive that horrific tragedy, without any parents within reach, in a sea of debris, for hours and hours, in a Third World environment, when my baby, here in the United States of America in a state-of-the-art facility with medical personnel galore, did not survive? Talk about not fair. Why was that child more important than mine was? I blurted my thoughts aloud before I could contain myself, and I found that a very uncomfortable silence followed. I realized that I probably should have kept quiet. No one understood.

Another change in me was more positive. I slowed down. Before Jacqueline, I had been, without a doubt, always running a hundred miles per hour. I had been a busy person, constantly finding things to do and places to go. I spent very little time just being, or just enjoying my home and my daughter. My cell phone had been glued to my ear; I was never willing to miss a call. "What if someone needs me?" I always thought. After Jacqueline and to this day, I feel that nothing was more important than my family. If my daughter or my son is with me, I rarely answered the phone. The call would not be about them, so who cared who needed me? I began understanding the fragility of life like nothing I had ever experienced. I enjoyed being home. Decorating my house became a pastime. Heather got me involved in choosing colors for my bare walls. We decorated everything—closets included!

Now I find that I want to spend time with my family. My priorities got clearer. I renewed my feelings for my husband, and we share many close times. I can even venture to say that we have gotten much closer since our loss.

I find that I mostly think of *that* day as the day that she was born rather than the day she died. I started feeling and thinking this way after the birth of my third child, Tristan. Somehow, from that point on, the glass was mostly always half full instead of half empty. These feelings are part of what I refer to as God's natural drug.

Christina's Birthday

Being around Veronique when there is an upcoming birthday party is a sight for sore eyes. The excitement of knowing that there will be a cake as well as birthday gifts to open is almost too much for her to handle. This is her most coveted dream. When Francine invited us to join their family to celebrate Christina's fourth birthday, we could not resist. However, my first thoughts were, "Can I go out of state to be a part of this celebration on the very day of my own daughter's second anniversary? Can I do that? Should I do that? What kind of person am I that I can leave my baby on such an important day?" These awful thoughts continuously crept into my brain, even though I tried very hard to block them.

These are the truths I know for sure; I know that leaving town for the weekend does not make me a bad person, or a bad mother, for that matter. I know logically that life must go on. In addition, I know that Jacqueline knows she is in my heart. It does not matter where I choose to be when I have her in my heart, right? I know all that. I know this for sure. So why do I still second-guess myself? I discussed it with Ken, and he was more than agreeable at the prospect of going. I am sure he was hoping that there would be less sadness on my part. That being with my family on the anniversary of her death would be helpful. We agreed to go.

On the morning of June 3, Ken discreetly took the kids out for a while. I was mostly just in a thinking mode. I was sad but not as much as I expected. The old saying "time heals all wounds" has some validity. I find this to be tremendously hard to admit, as I thought, for a long time, that I should mourn her forever, as a tribute or out of respect—you pick.

I kept wondering if the major sadness was just around the corner. I wondered if it was going to hit me, and hit me hard, soon. An hour later, Ken returned with a gift for me. Of course, Veronique could not contain herself and just had to open it for me. Inside the small box was a pearl necklace. A beautiful pearl necklace. Pearl is Jacqueline's birthstone. I was touched, very touched, by his gesture.

During the course of the day, again I found myself much happier than I expected. Being with a bunch of kids for a birthday party was a great distraction. I will admit that the day is a little bit of a blur to me, because I did have some unhappy thoughts. I thought of her grave and how I was not there, visiting it, bringing flowers. I will not lie to you and say that that day was easy. It was not. I wanted to lie down in my bed and just be there all day. I did not want to feel; I did not want to be. Mostly, I tried to push those thoughts out of my mind and try to enjoy the here and now.

I had thought that June 3 would forever be a very difficult date for me. That I would be a basket case forever more on that fateful date. I feel differently now. I almost feel the opposite now. I know that I was given a small gift—the gift of automatically being surrounded by my family on that day, especially being with my sister. There will always be a celebration for Christina's birthday. Her fifth, her sixth, her seventh, and so on. My parents will always be there to help in the celebration, and I can almost always be with them. Christina's birthday is a reason for being together on that date. I personally feel that I can have a small remembrance ceremony for Jacqueline as well, surrounded by the most important gift of all, my family.

Heather had given me a white balloon with a beautiful poem called "Little Angel" attached to it. I had it blown up that morning and, during the festivities, Ken, Veronique, Tristan and I went in Francine's backyard and had a very small dedication for our angel. Veronique was holding the balloon, and on cue, she let it go to the heavens to our angel.

I later received messages from both Heather and Susan, saying that they had visited the cemetery and offered flowers to my angel. What touching messages. I was honored. I know I did not thank them enough for going out of their way to do that, but I hoped they could hear what my heart was saying. Thank you. Thank you very much.

Conclusion

I never thought that something like this could happen to me. Losing my newborn child was unthinkable. I was one of those women who barely even thought about the possibility of having a first trimester miscarriage. I realize now that I took almost everything in my life for granted—until my loss, that is. Having Jacqueline changed me in so many ways. What is unbelievable is that I can honestly say that I am a happier person now. I would not have been able to say this just one year ago.

I feel that the death of my daughter Jacqueline had a purpose. Everyone needs a purpose in life. This is ultimately what makes life worth living. I will not kid you and say that there are not still difficult times—times when I feel, Why me? However, now I feel I have my answer. This great loss happened to me because my purpose was to make a difference. I am here to tell you that our lost babies should not be forgotten. I opened myself up to help you understand what goes through a grieving mother's mind. I know I am not alone. Others feel as I do.

This happened to me so I can help grieving mothers, fathers, friends, and family members heal by telling my story—by helping them understand that sometimes our living children need to know how we feel. Our children need to connect too. Through your own experience, you may find friends in unlikely places—friends you did not know existed. Accept them, as I did.

Since the birth of my third child, there is a softer side to me. I can now answer the basic "How many children do you have?" question without pearls of sweat rolling down my temples. If I feel like stating the accurate facts, I do, and if I feel that the question was asked in a polite, small-talk kind of way, then I may not mention my angel in heaven. Either way, I have come to terms with my answer. I know, without a doubt, that Jacqueline is watching and only wanting the best for me. God's natural drug, the most powerful positive influence, is still effectively working within me, healing me.

Quotes

My first reaction to this book was admiration for many reasons. Chantal has turned a tragic event into something positive as well as healing for many people, including me. Remembering Jacqueline was one of Chantal's main concerns. She did not want people to forget about her. I think that Chantal found a great way to get people to remember her daughter by helping others. I remember wondering why God chose the Hørups' daughter, and now I see why. Maybe they did not realize their strength until they were tested.

—Stacy Dragulescu

Even though I remember talking to Chantal about Jacqueline, I noticed that she confided in other friends more than she did me. The few times that I felt a true, intimate connection were when we went to church on Sundays. There, we both cried endlessly during the songs reminding us both of our experiences. I felt her pain so deeply and prayed for her anger and sorrow to lessen. There was no talking, just feeling the pain. That is what I could do for her. Stand by her and just feel.

—Bel Gallagher

When Chantal called me to let me know she was on her way to the birthing center, my first thought was that our daughters would share a birthday. Incredible! What are the odds? We had been joking about it throughout the whole pregnancy. Soon after I heard that Jacqueline died, I was hit with a depressing thought—Oh, my God! Jacqueline died on my daughter's birthday. How were we going to deal with this? How would Chantal ever be able to care for my daughter's birthday now that it means something so horrible and devastating? We had just started to really get to know each other, to really connect. We had something in common—our children. Now, that seemed tainted.

—Francine Delisle Paszkiewicz

Chantal was very social, open, full of life, strong-willed, very funny, "coquette" and she was so optimistic, so warm with a big, open heart. I will not say she is no longer like that, because she is, but there is the Chantal before Jacqueline's death and the Chantal after. The tragic loss of her newborn child changed her in many ways. In my opinion, Chantal has lost a lot of joy in her, a lot of life in her. However, she seems to have gained a deeper spiritual life, a more philosophical approach in her life, focusing only on what is important, on what matters for her and her immediate family, which I think is admirable. She is such a beautiful person inside and outside.

—Aude Femano

As the months grew on, ours became a wonderful friendship. Chantal is the kind of friend who will do anything for anyone, including telling you things you need to hear, but no one else will tell you. I can honestly say that I have become a better person and friend because of her. She has amazing strength and faith like none that I have ever seen.

—Heather Bender

Looking back, I realize how ridiculous these thoughts were, but at the time, they seemed perfectly normal. My thought was that Chantal should not go to the hospital that next day. She should not even see the baby, let alone hold her. For some reason in my screwed up brain, I actually thought if she never saw the baby, then it would be easier for her to cope with later. As if she could just pretend it never even happened. I realize now what a crazy, naive, absurd thought that was.

—Amy Iaquinta

As a pediatrician, I know that one of the hardest ordeals in life is dealing with the loss of your own child. It is one of life's unjustifiable events to outlive those which you have brought into this world. I feel Chantal's book is a great work to help, not only her, but also to help others deal with a tragic event. Through the process of grieving, one's personality and philosophy become altered. Sometimes this is for the better, sometimes for the worse. Chantal has decided to openly embrace the loss of Jacqueline through memorials, photo albums, and now this book. I hope, as well as she, that this can also help others deal with fatality, heal, and become better people to comfort and support others.

As a pediatrician, I highly recommend this exceptional book for all healthcare providers as a must-read!

—Lance S. Lowe, M.D.
Palmetto Pediatrics of the Lowcountry

"This remarkable book about loss and resilience is an inspiration to us all."

—Richeleen Schoonmaker, M.S., L.M.F.T.

978-0-595-44572-1
0-595-44572-1

Printed in the United States
94350LV00006B/46-48/A